SHAFTESBURY SCHOOL

LEARNING

SUPPORT CENTRE

A HIGHER REALITY

'The once great abbey of Shaftesbury, like so many Benedictine monasteries from Subiaco and Montecassino onwards, was built on a hill. It was a beacon to the county below. It symbolised a higher reality, an inspiration felt by us all.'

AIDAN BELLINGER

A HIGHER REALITY

THE HISTORY
OF SHAFTESBURY'S
ROYAL NUNNERY

JOHN CHANDLER

First published in the United Kingdom in 2003 by
The Hobnob Press, PO Box 1838, East Knoyle, Salisbury SP3 6FA
on behalf of the Friends of Shaftesbury Abbey, Park Walk, Shaftesbury SP7 8JR

British Library Cataloguing in Publication Data
A catalogue record for this book is available from the British Library.

ISBN 0-946418-14-4

Typeset in 11/16.5 pt Scala
Typesetting and origination by John Chandler
Printed in Great Britain by Salisbury Printing Company Ltd, Salisbury

Contents

Preface and
Acknowledgements

LAURA SYDENHAM's *Shaftesbury and its Abbey* was published in 1959 and reprinted in 1978. By the mid-1990s it was out of print and, with ambitious plans for new buildings and new displays at the abbey site, the Friends of Shaftesbury Abbey considered revising her book for another edition. In the event it was decided to commission a new work, and it was my honour and privilege to be entrusted with the enjoyable task of writing it.

The world of history has changed a great deal since 1959, and many of its branches that impinge on Shaftesbury Abbey – social, local, landscape, women's, monastic – have been revolutionized during the last forty years. Indeed a perusal of this book's bibliography will reveal a number of topics which (and authors who) had not been thought of in 1959. My involvement with Shaftesbury Abbey, other than the occasional visit to the ruins, precedes the writing of this book by a couple of years. I was asked to conduct some of the research for the text panels of the new displays, and became interested in the abbey's impressive history. Although much of my published output has concentrated on Wiltshire, I have frequently worked on Dorset topics and have always enjoyed the friendly co-operation and support of its local history providers and enthusiasts. And, since moving to East Knoyle in 1991, Shaftesbury has been my nearest town; so it is a great pleasure to try to repay, with this book, a little of the enjoyment that frequent visiting and using this very special place have brought me.

My book is intended to offer a brief, current and readable treatment of the history of Shaftesbury Abbey and, to a lesser extent, of the town with which its fortunes have been bound up. I hope it will be of interest therefore to Shastonians, and to everyone whose curiosity has been whetted by a visit to the abbey ruins and new museum. To make it useful also to specialists in monastic history I have supported the text with annotations (referenced to each substantial paragraph) and a considerable bibliography. I hope by this means that the book may offer a starting point for further research on the various topics it includes.

The writing of this book has engaged me intermittently during 2002 and the early part of 2003, and I took most of the photographs during January and February 2003. My research has been conducted in various libraries and record offices, and I owe a great debt to the staff of the following institutions: University of Southampton Library; University of Bristol Library; Brotherton Library, University of Leeds; Dorchester, Gillingham and Shaftesbury Libraries (Dorset County Council); Trowbridge and Salisbury Reference Libraries (Wiltshire County Council); Dorset Record Office; Wiltshire & Swindon Record Office; and Shaftesbury Town Museum. In addition Elinor Murphy has created an impressive reference collection of relevant books, papers and other material at Shaftesbury Abbey Museum, and I have been offered privileged use of this library. The small mountain of photocopies, photographs and notes which research for this book has created will shortly find its way there.

The illustrations in this book (apart from my own recent photographs) either belong to the Friends of Shaftesbury Abbey (as part of the museum library) or are the work of artists – Ronald Homes and Frank Garbutt – on the Friends' behalf. The illustration on page 60 from the Shaftesbury Psalter is reproduced with the permission of the British Library, and those of documents on pages 63, 82 and 97 with the permission of the Wiltshire & Swindon Record Office. I have tried not to infringe anyone's copyright, but if I have failed I apologize. In addition to my thanks to the two artists mentioned above, Ronald Homes and Frank Garbutt, I should also like to acknowledge David Cousins, who has designed this book's striking cover. All other aspects of the design and typesetting, including the preparation of the maps, have been my responsibility.

Various friends have helped me with specific points or general support, and I am most grateful to Joe Bettey, Corin Corley, Peter Cox, Douglas Crowley, Steve Hobbs and Ruth Smalley. The Friends of Shaftesbury Abbey have been encouraging, patient and (as their title suggests) friendly throughout this project, which has taken much longer than they anticipated. My thanks especially to Janet Bell, Keith Davies, Sheila Himmel, Sue Lobb, Mary Muir, Janet Patch, Julian Richards, and Jan and Jo Rutter. My greatest debts are to Anna McDowell, Chairman of the Friends, who commissioned the book; and to Elinor Murphy and Frank Hopton, the real historians of Shaftesbury Abbey, who with great courtesy and diligence have read each chapter as it was written, and have (usually) persuaded me to see the error of my ways. The book is dedicated to them. The mistakes that remain are very definitely mine.

John Chandler
East Knoyle
February 2003

Note: As this book was going to press King Alfred's restaurant, 17 High Street, which is mentioned several times in the text, announced that it was changing its name to Wharfe's.

1 Paladore

NO INLAND TOWN in southern England enjoys so dramatic a position as Shaftesbury. Here a lofty finger of greensand rock points westward, high above the flat clays of Blackmore Vale and the infant River Stour. Beyond the green mosaic of pastures the eye discerns softly sculpted distant hills, the chalk downlands of Dorset to the south and Wiltshire to the north. The dark wooded ridge of Selwood closes the western view, with all Somerset beyond. The striking prospect of such a citadel, not to mention the dramatic

The view to the south-west from Park Walk.

weather to which it is exposed – gales and mists, frosts and sunsets – imbues Shaftesbury with an unforgettable quality, a place of ancient mystery.

So it comes as no surprise to find a fanciful early history for Shaftesbury in the pages of medieval chroniclers – and a romantic name, 'the castle of Paladore'. The name, recalled by the Dorset authors Thomas Hardy and William Barnes, is largely forgotten here now, as is the eagle who prophesied while its wall was being built, and the king, Hudibras, its supposed founder. The medieval claim that it was built a thousand years before Christ (and shortly after Solomon built the temple) was already being questioned by Dorset's first historian, Thomas Gerard, in the 1620s. The euphonious 'Paladore' is the Welsh word for the shaft of a spear, and so is a simple translation of the English name. In fact, the 'shaft' in Shaftesbury is most probably not an allusion to anything shaft-like, such as the steep hills or vanished church spires, but is derived from a Saxon personal name, *Sceaft*.[1]

Shaftesbury's history in fact begins around the year 880, with the establishment by King Alfred of a town and nunnery here. At least, that has been the view of most historians from Gerard onwards. It will be well, therefore, to begin by examining this claim, and trying to discover what was here before Alfred.

Some two centuries of archaeological endeavour have failed to establish whether Shaftesbury hill, like its fellow sentinels overlording Blackmore – Hambledon, Hod Hill, Buzbury, Whitesheet, and (perhaps) Duncliffe – was fortified in prehistory. It would have made an excellent hillfort. Perhaps all trace of iron-age defences across the promontory have been destroyed by later settlement, or perhaps they remain to be found. Meanwhile the only prehistoric finds from the vicinity of Shaftesbury have been pits containing flint and pottery debris excavated near Mampitts Lane (north-east of the town) in 1949–50; and some flints, of possible prehistoric date, found at Old Barn House, north-west of Bimport, in 1947. So at present the archaeological record cannot sustain any theory of a prehistoric fortification.[2]

Nor is there any compelling evidence for a Saxon settlement on the hill before Alfred. The name presumably existed before it was used for the new town, so *Sceaft* or one of his predecessors perhaps fortified the hill ('–bury' derives from a Saxon word for a fortified place) during a period of danger, real or

Shaftesbury in the context of Saxon Wessex.

imagined. In peaceful times a lower-lying site, close to a water supply, would be preferred. The settlement pattern in the adjacent Dorset and Wiltshire countryside during the later Saxon period – as seen in the present-day distribution of villages – favours valleys and rivers so, unless for defence, there is no reason why anyone should decide to make their home on Shaftesbury's hill.[3]

That Shaftesbury was not an important place before Alfred's time seems to be confirmed when one looks at the pattern of territorial boundaries nearby. By the ninth century a network of so-called 'central places' had been established which acted as religious centres, and often had administrative and trading functions as well. Such places possessed a minster, a church to which a community of priests was attached, and they were responsible for evangelising the population in a defined block of the surrounding countryside. These 'minster parishes', as their lands are known, dovetailed across north Dorset and south Wiltshire, but the site of Shaftesbury, far from being the focus and centre of such a territory, actually lay close to the meeting of three, based on Gillingham, Iwerne (Minster) and Tisbury. All three of these early-established centres were later to cede possessions to Alfred's new foundation at Shaftesbury.[4]

Probable minster territories in the Shaftesbury area (after Hall 2000).

The local communities whose territory impinged on the area of modern Shaftesbury must have included Melbury Abbas to the south and Motcombe to the north. Motcombe was subordinate to Gillingham, and lay within the royal forest. One of its hamlets, Enmore Green, seems to have developed at the forest edge during the middle ages below Shaftesbury's hill, and was the major source of the town's water supply; but there is no indication that a settlement existed there in the Saxon period. But Melbury from an early date probably had dependent settlements at Cann and perhaps also in the St James area, immediately below the Shaftesbury promontory. A glimpse of the pre-urban

Enmore Green, viewed from Castle Hill.

landscape (although dating in fact from several decades after Shaftesbury's foundation) is offered in one of the abbey's Saxon charters, which describes a small farming territory within the Cann portion of Melbury. Although interpretations differ it could have extended from the low-lying area around Watery Lane and French Mill south of Shaftesbury up on to part of the hill (then called Brand's Ridge) on which the medieval and modern town sits. In defining the traditional bounds of the land involved its charter takes no account of the recent arrival of the abbey and town on the same hilltop.[5]

Alfred is the best known and best documented of a series of kings who, during the ninth and tenth centuries, extended their West-Saxon power base across the whole of southern England and into the Midlands. This they achieved in the teeth of repeated harassment and invasion attempts by Viking warlords who controlled much of eastern England. As a warrior King Alfred is remembered for a victory in 878 – near Edington in west Wiltshire – which dissuaded the Vikings from further adventures for more than a decade and, seen with hindsight, tipped the power balance in favour of Wessex. But great rulers are more than warriors, and Alfred deserves his title for his activities off the battlefield – as a lawmaker, administrator, scholar and religious reformer. Two of Alfred's innovations were directly responsible for the existence of Shaftesbury.[6]

After his victory in 878 Alfred put his kingdom in readiness for further attacks. He designated a chain of 'safe places' – existing towns which could be fortified, some earlier fortifications for re-use (including prehistoric hillforts), and some entirely new creations. Each was to serve as a place of last resort for the inhabitants of their surrounding countryside, who were responsible for maintaining its defences and providing its garrison. The details of this ambitious plan, which combined civil defence with town planning, are recorded in a document known as the *Burghal Hidage* (because it lists the fortified places – *burhs* – and the number of family landholdings – hides – assigned to each of them). This document, which dates from the very end of Alfred's reign, 899, or slightly later, has been much discussed in recent years, and many of its obscurities illuminated.[7]

Shaftesbury is one of four Dorset places listed, the others being Christchurch (formerly in Hampshire), Wareham, and Bridport. In neighbouring counties its nearest counterparts were Wilton and Langport. Its responsibility, for 700 hides, must have embraced all of Blackmore Vale and north Dorset, perhaps together with neighbouring areas of Wiltshire and Somerset. If our previous assumptions are correct, Shaftesbury was a new foundation and not (like Malmesbury, whose position it somewhat resembles) an old town refortified. As a new town it should be compared with another of the Dorset *burhs*, Wareham, and with very similar constructions at Cricklade in Wiltshire, Wallingford in Oxfordshire (formerly Berkshire), and Lydford in Devon.[8]

Despite the similarities in plan between the new foundations there is no indication that they were all established at the same time. And taking the *Burghal Hidage* places as a whole they show a great diversity – of size, position and layout. Nor do we know to what extent the systematic coverage which the list implies was ever implemented or tested. It may be merely a blueprint of good intentions which was only partly accomplished. That said, there is a second piece of evidence which, if it can be taken at face value, would suggest that Shaftesbury was one of the first, if not the first, of the new towns to be built, and was thus in some respects the prototype.[9]

A scrap of paper now displayed in Shaftesbury Town Museum and dating from 1904 or later may seem strange confirmation of a visit to Shaftesbury nearly 800 years earlier. The visitor, before 1125, was the foremost historian of his day, William of Malmesbury, and he recorded seeing an inscribed stone in the abbey chapter house which had come from an old ruined wall. In Latin it proclaimed: 'King Alfred built this town in the eighth year of his reign, AD 880'. In 1904 a fragment of this inscribed stone was found during the excavations of the abbey church, and a rubbing was made on paper. The stone

Rubbing on paper of an inscription, perhaps that recording the town's foundation.

has since been lost again, but the rubbing remains. The way in which the letters of the inscription have been formed suggests that it does not in itself date from 880, but from a century or so later. It may have been cut to adorn a new town wall, constructed perhaps at a time of emergency around 1001. And there is a small problem with the date. Alfred came to the throne in April 871, so the year 880 straddled the ninth and tenth years of his reign, not the eighth.[10]

Strictly speaking, the stone is not evidence that the town of Shaftesbury was founded in 880, but that there was a tradition a century or so later that 880 was the foundation date. More importantly, perhaps, it suggests that, when Shaftesbury was still relatively new, people believed that it was older than the abbey, since the traditional date for the abbey's foundation (which will be considered shortly) is around 888. And that is what is implied, too, by Alfred's biographer, Asser, who claimed that the abbey was built 'next to the east gate of Shaftesbury'. In other words we should think of the town and abbey as separate foundations, the plan of the town not necessarily including any provision for the slightly later abbey.[11]

Alfred's defensive scheme envisaged that each hide would supply one man to garrison the *burh's* defences, and that they should be deployed at intervals of approximately 1.3 metres (4 feet) around the ramparts. It is possible, therefore, to calculate from the *Burghal Hidage* the intended circuit of each town's defences. Shaftesbury's 700 hides could garrison a rampart 880 metres (962 yards). This is quite insufficient to encompass the whole of the promontory as far east as the present town so, unless the steepest portions of the escarpment were regarded as naturally insurmountable and were left undefended, we should look for a rampart further west. Remains of such an earthwork crossing the hilltop have been detected as a slight but continuous rise in ground level along what is now Magdalene Lane, to the west of the abbey site, where the present Westminster Hospital is approached. A rectangle formed by

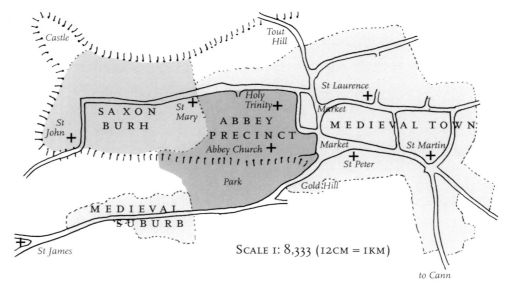

Saxon and medieval elements within the town plan of Shaftesbury (based on Penn 1980).

Magdalene Lane on the east and the top of the escarpment on the other three sides (excluding the protruding site of the medieval castle) gives the required circumference length fairly accurately. A very similar arrangement is to be found at another of Alfred's new *burhs*, Lydford in Devon, where the Saxon defended town occupies only part of a dramatic promontory. At Lydford it has been shown by excavation that the defences continued along the top of the steepest slopes. At Shaftesbury an eastern defence along Magdalene Lane would accord with Asser's description of the subsequent abbey's position, which was built next to the east gate of the town.[12]

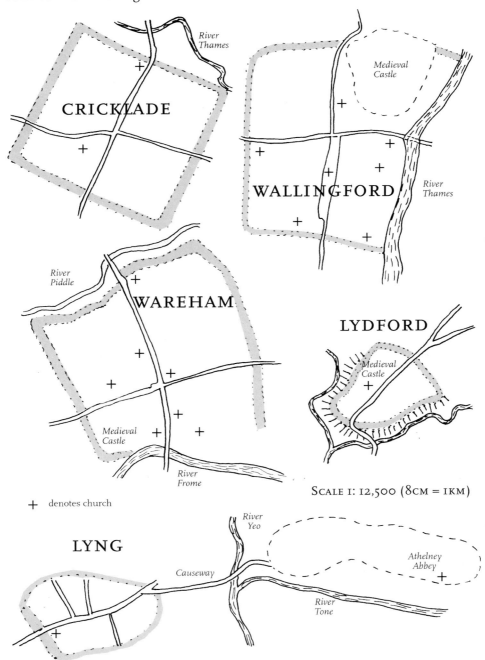

Simplified sketch plans of Burghal Hidage towns (based on Haslam 1984a).

If the original town of
Shaftesbury stood at the western end
of the promontory, then it is possible to
detect vestiges of its internal arrangement which correspond closely to
Alfred's other new towns. Bimport
would have been the main street,
bisecting the rectangle into northern
and southern halves. The name means
'within the town' or 'the market
within', and has a direct parallel at
Malmesbury. Love Lane, Magdalene
Lane and the upper part of St John's
Hill would follow the line of original
streets running along inside the
ramparts. A similar intra-mural street

Three views of the site of Saxon Shaftesbury: (top) Magdalene Lane looking north across
Bimport, the site of the east gate; (above) the north-eastern corner of the town looking across
Castle Hill; (right) St John's Hill, the south-western exit.

line is seen at Cricklade, Winchester and elsewhere. Langfords Lane and some
of the many surviving property boundaries trending north–south across the
promontory on either side of Bimport may represent original divisions within
the Saxon town. And, most significantly, the two likely entrances to the town, an
east gate where Magdalene Lane meets Bimport, and a west gate where St
John's Hill turns and begins its steep descent, were both the sites of medieval
churches, St Mary's and St John's. Churches over or beside town entrances were
very characteristic features of *Burghal Hidage* towns, and their medieval
successors survive, for example, at Langport, Cricklade and Chisbury. St
Martin's at Wareham, in a similar position, retains Saxon fabric.[13]

The chain of *Burghal Hidage* forts which Alfred planned and
implemented for the physical welfare of his subjects is paralleled by a second
innovation, designed to secure their spiritual welfare. The study and observance
of religion lay at the heart of Alfred's own personal philosophy, and influenced
his ideas of kingship and good governance. But the notion of devout rulers and
God-fearing subjects extended beyond political theory. The neglect of religious
values was seen as incurring God's displeasure, whose punishment was the
Viking invasions. Religious revival, seen in these terms, was as much a strategy
for national security, therefore, as were the *Burghal Hidage* forts. One plank of
Alfred's policy was religious education, including the translation of key Latin
texts into the vernacular English; another was establishing and renewing
monastic houses.[14]

The monastic ideal, of men and women retiring from secular life and
devoting themselves to the service of God, in prayer and worship, can be traced
back to the eastern Roman empire in the third and fourth centuries. In Egypt
the desert fathers, solitaries living out their lives as hermits singly or in loosely
affiliated groups, set the model for similar individuals and communities who
withdrew to remote places along the western fringes of Britain and Ireland from
the fifth century onwards. This Celtic form of monasticism persisted and
spread, but with the evangelization of lowland England from Rome during the
sixth and seventh centuries these communities gradually adopted Roman
forms of worship and practice. At the same time many new monasteries, on the
Roman pattern, were established, and these became the powerhouses behind
the spread of Christianity throughout Britain. In Wessex places such as

Dorchester on Thames, Winchester, Malmesbury, Sherborne, Glastonbury and Crediton were important early monastic centres, many associated with the work of a charismatic individual, such as Birinus, Aldhelm or Boniface. But the Viking raids and invasions of the ninth century virtually extinguished monastic life in England and, although many of the towns and other places in which they had existed continued as important centres of trade, administration and religion, most traces of the early monasteries have disappeared. It is these early missionary monasteries that underlie some (but not all) of the high-status churches later enountered as minsters – which is of course a variation of the same word. Tisbury had an early monastery, and so did Iwerne. But if our reasoning earlier in this chapter is correct, Shaftesbury did not.[15]

In his biography of Alfred, Asser tells us that the king established two new monasteries, a house for monks at Athelney in Somerset, and a house for nuns at Shaftesbury. He does not give us a date for these foundations, but it is likely to have been between 887 and 893. Later medieval chroniclers guessed at 888, and they cannot have been far wrong. Such an enterprise would have taken some time, in any case, to accomplish.[16]

Why Athelney, why Shaftesbury? Athelney is the easier to understand. An island of high ground surrounded by the swampy moors of the Somerset Levels, it was the place from which Alfred in 878 had rallied his forces to begin the successful campaign against the Vikings. It had royal associations – the name means 'island of the princes' – and there were royal estates around it, at North Curry and Martock, to contribute to the monastery's endowment. The founding of a monastery there could be presented as, and probably was, a thank-offering to God for deliverance when Wessex fortunes were at their lowest ebb. It was, moreover, adjacent to a *Burghal Hidage* fort, at Lyng, to which it was connected by a causeway and bridge, and so could be defended.[17]

Shaftesbury, too, may have been a significant place in Alfred's 878 campaign. It was close to the mustering point – a lost landmark called Egbert's Stone – of the Wessex forces from Somerset, Wiltshire and western Hampshire, which marched to victory at Edington. Following that victory it may have been, as we discussed earlier, one of the first places to have been fortified from scratch within what became the *Burghal Hidage* scheme. Furthermore land from the defunct monasteries at Tisbury and Iwerne was available as an endowment.[18]

Like Athelney, Shaftesbury may have been built as a thank offering. Asser tells us only that Alfred put his daughter Aethelgifu, in charge of the house; but in doing so he was emulating a Northumbrian king, Oswiu, who more than two centuries earlier, in 655, dedicated an infant daughter to the religious life in return for success over an enemy. Alfred would have known about Oswiu, and he had himself visited a nunnery at Brescia in Lombardy, on his way to Rome thirty years earlier, which had been founded with the king's daughter as abbess. So Shaftesbury Abbey, whatever the larger intention, provided a means whereby Alfred provided for one of his daughters, who would from infancy have been destined for the veil (as we shall see in chapter 2). In a similar fashion he appointed another member of the household, his former teacher John the Old Saxon, as abbot of Athelney.[19]

There are no statues of Alfred in Shaftesbury, as there are in some other towns associated with him. True, he lurks in the name of a school and a restaurant, but there is not even a street named in his honour. And yet, unlike Wantage, Winchester and Pewsey, whose squares his image graces, Shaftesbury can claim him as its founder – were it not for Alfred there is no particular reason why the place would have ever existed.

2 A Group of Noble Dames

ARESIDENCE SUITABLE FOR NUNS is the English translation of Asser's phrase describing Alfred's foundation at Shaftesbury. What sort of nuns, and what sort of residence, are the large questions with which this chapter will be concerned. But these matters must be set against the background of Saxon monasticism generally, on the one hand, and also, more specifically, within the narrower confines of Shaftesbury's hill and the Saxon population who lived there.[1]

Of the English monasteries which existed (and had mostly disappeared) before Shaftesbury was founded at least thirty, and probably more than sixty, included religious women as well as men. There do not appear to have been any nunneries as such, but there were double houses of men and women, more or less segregated, under the control of an abbess. The nature of these religious communes, as we might term them, probably varied; some – perhaps all – functioned also as minsters, offering an evangelising and pastoral role to the population living in the countryside outside their precincts. Double houses were based on a model widespread in continental Europe, and are known to have existed in Kent, the south Midlands and Thames Valley, and in Northumbria. In Wessex they seem to have been very rare, with only two well documented foundations, at Wareham and Wimborne, both in Dorset.[2]

Like their counterparts in Kent both these Dorset houses were linked to royalty. Wimborne was associated with St Cuthburga, sister of King Ine (688–

710); and at Wareham, which may have been founded for a daughter of King Centwine (676–685), King Beorhtric was buried in 802. The status of nunneries, as we shall see, reflected the status of women in society, so that communities founded for or by royal women were regarded as royal possessions under royal protection. The disappearance of the Saxon double houses, it has been suggested, may reflect the fate of the various royal factions which had supported them, rather than their actual destruction at Viking hands. Because of Alfred's success against the Vikings both Wimborne and Wareham were able to survive longer than most double houses elsewhere, and were probably still functioning when Shaftesbury was founded in the 880s. But both had been associated with Alfred's dynastic rivals, and both ceased to be monastic houses in the tenth century.[3]

Alfred's innovation in founding Shaftesbury Abbey was not that he created a monastic house for a female member of his family – in this he was following a long tradition – but that he initiated the idea of a house for nuns alone, a nunnery. Male brethren had to be associated with the house, to officiate as priests at religious services, but they were not living as monks in a double community. Shaftesbury was a nunnery for nuns, the counterpart of Athelney, a monastery for monks. Athelney's success was limited – it was rapidly eclipsed by its neighbour, Glastonbury – but Shaftesbury prospered. That it was an effective and impressive role-model can best be seen in the later nunneries which it inspired. The first was the so-called Nunnaminster at Winchester, which was later known as St Mary's Abbey. It may have been planned before Alfred's death in 899 and was implemented by his widow Ealhswith, who died before 905. Very soon afterwards, perhaps c.907, another nunnery was founded nearby, at Romsey, by Alfred's successor, Edward the Elder; and Wilton Abbey may also have originated during his reign, although it claimed to date back to Alfred's time or before. Then, towards the end of the tenth century, Queen Aelfthryth, whom we shall encounter in chapter 3, was responsible for two further nunneries, at Amesbury in Wiltshire and Wherwell in north Hampshire. All five of these houses, like Shaftesbury, were royal nunneries, in that they had close links with the ruling dynasties, and included noble and royal women among the members of their communities. They played host to kings and queens, and it was in Shaftesbury Abbey that King Cnut died in 1035. As a

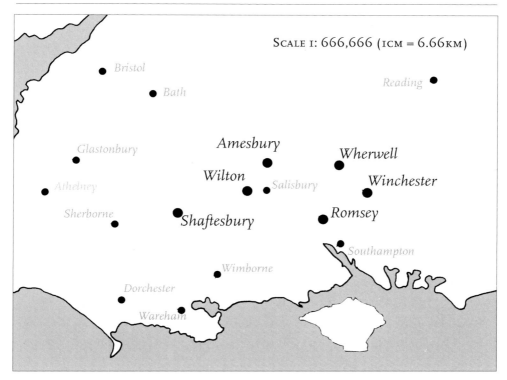

SCALE I: 666,666 (1CM = 6.66KM)

Bristol

Bath

Reading

Glastonbury

Amesbury

Wherwell

Atheney

Wilton

Salisbury

Winchester

Sherborne

Shaftesbury

Romsey

Southampton

Wimborne

Dorchester

Wareham

The six Wessex nunneries in the context of major towns and monasteries.

group they clustered in a relatively small area of southern England, beyond which only four Saxon nunneries were founded, and they all continued as important religious and estate centres right up to their dissolution in the sixteenth century.[4]

About Aethelgifu, the first abbess of Shaftesbury, we know disappointingly little. She was Alfred's third surviving child, and since he married in 868, it can be assumed that she was no more than a teenager when her abbey was founded in about 888. The decision that she was to become a nun would have been made for her when she was still an infant, either for political reasons (to prevent her from diluting the royal line by producing sons), or – as a not wholly reliable source explains – because she was of delicate health. Since Asser, Alfred's biographer, describes her as 'a virgin subject and consecrated to the rules of monastic life' at the time of her appointment as abbess, it may be assumed that she had already been brought up in a monastic environment, probably at one of the two known double houses in Wessex – Wimborne or

Wareham. She is mentioned in Alfred's will, perhaps drawn up in the 880s, but since the bequests of land to her do not seem to have taken effect, it has been suggested that she may have predeceased her father. At any rate she was not a sufficiently charismatic pioneer for her to be regarded as a saint after her death.[5]

We know of other royal Saxon women associated with Shaftesbury. St Aelfgifu was the queen of King Edmund, the mother of Kings Edwy and Edgar, and therefore the grandmother of Edgar's sons, Edward the Martyr and Aethelred. She died here in 944, and the similarity of her name to that of Alfred's daughter, Aethelgifu, has led to confusion. William of Malmesbury, apparently rolling the two into one, claimed that Aelfgifu had founded the nunnery. In fact she seems merely to have come to Shaftesbury as an invalid and died here. William wrote a poem in her honour, which begins: 'Long anguished by the pain of sickness dire . . .' Her importance to the nunnery was that her tomb became a focus for veneration by pilgrims, where healing miracles were performed, and so she was soon regarded as a saint. Although eclipsed at Shaftesbury later in the century by her grandson St Edward, her cult continued locally throughout the middle ages. She was honoured elsewhere until at least the twelfth century, and a relic of her body was venerated in Exeter Cathedral.[6]

Aelfgifu's choice of Shaftesbury can be explained by the presence here of her mother, Wynflaed, and possibly also her mother-in-law, Eadgifu. Neither they nor she can have been nuns in the fullest sense, of virgins devoted to God. If they had made a commitment to the monastic life, as descriptions used of them such as 'religious woman' and 'servant of God' would imply, then they were vowesses – wives or widows who had made a vow of chastity to debar themselves from remarriage. Such women might retain land and property, and the liberty to travel beyond the abbey precinct; but they were linked to the abbey, which supported them in spiritual and practical ways, and which they in turn supported as benefactresses. We know the names, but nothing more, of two abbesses – Herelufu and Leofgifu – as well as three other women associated with Saxon Shaftesbury Abbey, as nuns or vowesses, because land that later accrued to the abbey had been previously given to them as a kind of dowry. Beorhtwyn, Aelfthryth and Brihtgifu may not have been royalty, but they, and doubtless many others like them, were drawn from the landowning Wessex aristocracy; their sojourn at the abbey was paid for with a portion of their families' estates.[7]

The royal connection with the nunneries operated in various ways, and because they were an innovation of Alfred's time we can see it evolving during the tenth century. They began as an adjunct of the court, a safe and secure home for royal and noble ladies, set apart from the turbulence of manly kingship. As such their roles might have included finishing school, nursing home, harem even. But this practical existence must be set alongside a revival in the ideals of monasticism and the creation of new monasteries, which (arguably) began with Alfred's reforms and accelerated under his successors, especially after Glastonbury was refounded in 940. Under an agreement drawn up in 973 during the reign of Edgar the English monasteries and nunneries all adopted the Benedictine rule. A version of the rule was drawn up for nuns, and nunneries were placed under the protection of the reigning queen. In theory, and probably in practice, their adoption of a stricter Benedictine monasticism distanced the nunneries from the outside world and from unwelcome interference by factions of the royal household, while enabling them to continue their educational and caring roles. This emancipation is most clearly seen in a changing attitude to landholding. Prior to Edgar's reign women, including members of a nunnery, were regarded as having only a life interest in the property which supported them, so that after a nun's death her endowment might be taken away from her nunnery. After the 973 agreement this practice ceased, so that Shaftesbury and the other nunneries could build up with confidence that stock of communal landholdings which would ensure their survival for another five centuries and more.[8]

Perhaps reflecting the impermanence of their possessions, none of the Wessex nunneries has a genuine foundation charter listing the estates which made up their original endowment. Asser, his biographer, tells us vaguely that, 'Alfred abundantly endowed these two monasteries [Athelney and Shaftesbury] with estates of land and every kind of wealth'. At Shaftesbury the absence of any 'starting-point' for its estate holdings seems to have been keenly felt, and two forged documents exist, purporting to date from the reigns of Alfred himself and his grandson Edwy (955–9). They are attempts to second-guess what such a charter might have included, based on the estates that the abbey possessed later.

The modern historian has to work in much the same way as the medieval forger, working back from Domesday Book and taking into account a number of genuine bequests and grants that have survived from the Saxon era.[9]

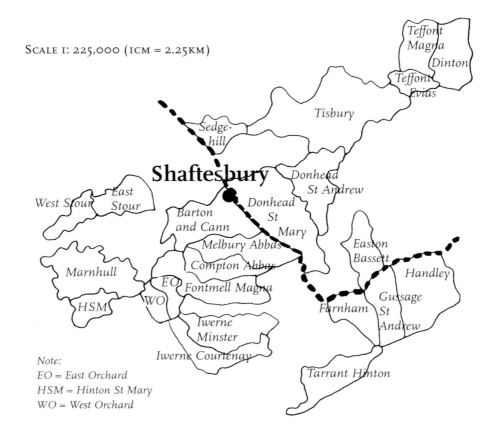

SCALE 1: 225,000 (1CM = 2.25KM)

Note:
EO = East Orchard
HSM = Hinton St Mary
WO = West Orchard

Abbey landholdings near Shaftesbury in the Saxon period. The estate boundaries, based on later parish boundaries, are approximate. The dotted line is the county boundary between Dorset (south and west) and Wiltshire (north and east).

Shaftesbury Abbey's landholdings in 1066, according to Domesday Book, lay mostly in north Dorset and south Wiltshire, with outliers on Purbeck, around Bradford on Avon, near Swindon and in west Sussex. They will be described in more detail in chapter 6. Measured in hides (nominal households) only about one-third of the total landholding of 369 hides in 1066 can be ascribed to a particular donor, date or circumstance. Estates at Fontmell Magna and Tarrant Hinton, for example, were granted to the abbey in 932 and 935, and we find land at East or West Orchard in 939, and on Purbeck in 948, in the possession of women who may well have been Shaftesbury nuns. We have conjectured that Alfred's original endowment included the estates of two early Saxon minsters/ monasteries, at Iwerne and Tisbury, which had disappeared and whose lands had reverted to the crown. This might account for the important Wiltshire estates of Tisbury, Donhead and Dinton, and some of the Dorset territory south of Shaftesbury. A third former minster, at Bradford on Avon in west Wiltshire, with very valuable lands, was granted to Shaftesbury in 1001 to serve as a refuge for the nuns and their relics of St Edward in the event of a Viking raid on north Dorset. This acquisition is further discussed below and in chapter 3.[10]

It would be pleasant to be able to describe the church in which Aethelgifu and her fellow nuns prayed, the cloister where they walked and the rooms in which they studied, ate and slept. But we cannot, since at present there is virtually no archaeological evidence for the earliest phases of the abbey's existence. A few fragments of architectural stonework earlier than the Norman

Saxon carved stonework, perhaps fragments of a cross.

conquest imply that by then some of the buildings were stonebuilt. One may be part of a Saxon cross-shaft. One plinth stone and the base of a pilaster buttress remain at the base of the north chapel which can be interpreted as survivors from a pre-conquest apsidal chancel. There are also four graveslabs. But that is all. Nor are historical sources of much use. Asser is at pains to emphasize that Alfred attracted numerous craftsmen of the highest competence to his retinue and that he endowed his two monasteries with land and wealth. But he does not explicitly say that the skilled craftsmen built Shaftesbury Abbey.[11]

So, faced with a lack of direct evidence about Shaftesbury, we must look elsewhere for comparisons. Athelney is the obvious starting point, since it was Shaftesbury's twin. The church here was of wooden construction, of moderate size and surrounded by the monks' dwellings. William of Malmesbury described the design of the church as innovatory, a square or rectangular atrium, with apsidal chancels or chapels leading off from all four sides. Such an arrangement suggests that Alfred had turned away from English antecedents and was looking to the continent, since there are parallels from Carolingian Europe. There, for some sixty years prior to the construction of Athelney and Shaftesbury, monasteries had been built to a blueprint, the St Gall plan, which introduced the idea of a cloister adjacent to a single monastic church, and with buildings for communal eating and sleeping. Such a plan will be familiar, of course, to anyone who has visited the remains of a medieval monastery, but it appears that Athelney and Shaftesbury may have been transitional in design, the conduit which brought the standard monastic plan to England.[12]

Behind the guildhall in Winchester, and close to King Alfred's statue, the excavations of a small portion of the Nunnaminster (St Mary's Abbey) remain exposed to view. The 1981–3 excavations revealed three main building phases. First a wooden church was built with a nave and a west front ending in apsidal north and south ends. This church, the excavators suggested, may also have had apsidal transepts and chancel, so would have been rather similar to William's description of Athelney. To this church probably also belonged 'a very high tower', which a chronicler tells us was dedicated in 908. The wooden church did not last long; by about 970 it was described as ruinous and was replaced by a much larger complex of stone buildings, including a new church that overlay the old. This in turn succumbed to a grander rebuilding scheme during the twelfth century.[13]

Excavations carried out at Romsey Abbey during the 1970s and in 1991, although inconclusive as to the relationship of early features, seem to paint a similar picture. The abbey, it will be recalled, was founded in about 907, and from this phase graves were discovered and two parallel rammed chalk and flint structures, which may have been the footings of the side walls of a timber church. Romsey Abbey was refounded in c.970 during the monastic revival of Edgar's reign, and it seems that the church was rebuilt about then in stone, using limestone from the Isle of Wight and some reused Roman building material. Parts of both transepts were encountered during the modern excavations, but reflooring inside the present Norman church a century ago had already revealed evidence for the Saxon nave and apsidal east end as well as the transepts.[14]

One further line of comparison relates not to the Saxon nunneries, but to churches which were built or adapted to contain relics. This is pertinent because, not only could Saxon Shaftesbury boast the relics of Aelfgifu after 944 and Edward the Martyr after 979, but it may also have possessed a portion of the True Cross. Such a relic had been given by the Pope to King Alfred in 883, who could have bestowed it on Shaftesbury at its consecration. Much later there is a reference in a will of 1015 to the abbey's dedication as the Holy Cross and St Edward, and there is still a Holyrood Farm close to the site of the abbey. In continental Europe prized relics were often kept safely in a crypt beneath the church, where pilgrims might venerate them; and there are also Saxon reliquary crypts in England, notably at Repton in Derbyshire and Wing near Aylesbury, although none is known in Wessex. It has been suggested that the first Shaftesbury Abbey church may have included a crypt to house its relics.[15]

The preservation of relics was given at the time (1001) as the reason for Shaftesbury's acquisition of the large and lucrative estate of Bradford on Avon in west Wiltshire. Here was to be built the abbey's refuge, should Viking invaders threaten the community, and here was to be maintained a cell of nuns as an outpost to the mother house. In the event we have no evidence that the nuns and their relics ever fled to safety in Bradford, but the position of churches there is suggestive. A major late-medieval parish church, believed to be the successor to the Saxon minster church which the nuns were granted, stands a stone's throw from the surviving Saxon chapel of St Lawrence, one of the gems

The Saxon chapel of St Lawrence, Bradford on Avon.

of pre-conquest architecture. Such a building, it has been suggested, small and without a nave, but richly ornamented outside and in, may have been built as the church of the nuns' cell, apart from but adjacent to the minster church. As such perhaps it gives us a glimpse of what, on a larger scale, Saxon Shaftesbury Abbey church may have looked like.[16]

If we stand back from these hints and analogies, and try to imagine Shaftesbury Abbey during the first two centuries of its existence, we must concede that the evidence is very flimsy. There is no reason why it should have looked like Athelney, or developed like Romsey, or appeared as a grander version of Bradford on Avon. But we can be reasonably confident that Shaftesbury Abbey was not static, that it evolved during this period. Perhaps, like its counterparts, it began as a complex of wooden buildings, loosely designed for communal living. And as it developed and grew wealthier, and more crowded with nuns and vowesses (and their households and retainers), it doubtless required larger premises, ornate structures of finely carved masonry. The new buildings may have reflected the more rigorous application of the Benedictine rule ushered in by the monastic revival, and the layout of the new monasteries that were springing up accordingly. The accumulation of important relics may have required special arrangements for their safety, such as the creation of a crypt. And the celebrity surrounding Edward's translation and his progress to sainthood (described in the next chapter) may have impacted, not only on the community of nuns, but also on the wider urban society outside its gates.

Here is one more topic for speculation which must be addressed. In the previous chapter we described the foundation of Shaftesbury as a *Burghal Hidage* town, and located it on the promontory to the west of the abbey campus. That is not where modern Shaftesbury stands. Modern (and medieval) Shaftesbury is focussed to the east of the abbey, on High Street and the Commons, and the roads leading to them. Documentary and comparative evidence hints that this change was occurring during the late tenth and eleventh centuries, while the nunnery was accruing relics and prestige, estates and recruits.

Shaftesbury's northern promontory from the north-west, with the open area of Castle Hill, the site of the original Saxon town.

First there is the evidence of a Saxon charter relating to land which later passed to the abbey. In 958 the king granted to a friend a small estate which has been equated with, or impinged upon, the later parish of St Peter's, a parish which in medieval times took in a large part of Shaftesbury town centre. The grant is couched in agricultural terms – fields, meadows, pastures, woods – and there is no suggestion that the land included any urban features. But a century later we learn from Domesday Book that Shaftesbury by then consisted of two manors, one belonging to the king, the other to the abbess. In 1066 the king's manor contained 104 houses, and the abbey's 153 houses. Both, for a reason so far unexplained, were greatly reduced during the twenty years after the conquest, so that in 1086 the king's manor had 66 houses, the abbess's 111. Then, about forty years later, William of Malmesbury made the puzzling remark that, 'Shaftesbury used to be a city (*urbs*) but is now a village (*vicus*)'.[17]

On reflection this evidence is not quite so perplexing. While there is no certainty that the two manors were entirely distinct and distinguishable on the ground, it is likely that the king owned the land within the old fortified burh on the promontory, while the abbess owned the land around it, as part of her 'home' manor later known as Barton or Cann. Whatever happened immediately after the conquest it struck the king's manor harder than the abbess's, and it may have involved clearance of houses for a castle, which was by the twelfth century in existence at the north-western tip of the promontory. If we may equate the abbess's manor with the settlement which developed into the present town then it was already more populous than the old burh by 1066, and still (despite the setback) had over one hundred houses in 1086 – making it one of the largest towns in Dorset.

So why did William call it a village? The answer perhaps lies in the meaning of the Latin word *vicus*. This term was often loosely used to signify village, but its true connotation was a collection of dwellings, extended to mean a row of houses, a street, or a neighbourhood. In other words William may have been telling us that, in place of the compact citadel of the burh, for which *urbs* would be the correct Latin description, Shaftesbury by his time had become something much looser and more spread out.[18]

This impression is reinforced if we consider the positions of Shaftesbury's churches. Away from the promontory there were at least nine during the middle ages – three in the St James area to the south, two on the High Street, one at each end of Salisbury Street, and two along the line of Bell Street/ Barton Street to the east. We cannot trace the history of any of these churches back to the Saxon period, but urban studies in England generally have shown that towns founded after the Norman conquest usually have only ever had one, or at most two, parish churches; whereas in Saxon towns churches with small parishes tended to proliferate. This, coupled with the negative evidence of the Saxon charter, is a good indication that the establishment of a settlement on abbey land east and south of Shaftesbury's promontory took place after 958 and before 1066. And the siting of its churches suggests that it began in linear fashion, perhaps sporadically along the main routes to and past the abbey precinct – the later St James's Street, Salisbury Street, High Street and Bell Street. Between these nodal points there was plenty of space for the medieval town to develop and grow, just as within the abbey precinct the Saxon plan could give way under the Normans to a far more magnificent complex of buildings.[19]

So we have brought the history of Shaftesbury and its abbey, albeit with many uncertainties and speculations, up to the Norman conquest. We have portrayed a dynamic, wealthy and prestigious Saxon community. But before we explore the medieval nunnery we must step back, to consider one of its most important – and strangest – possessions.

Stained glass roundel in the shrine of St Edward, designed and executed by Rupert Moore.

3 *Edwardstow*

I N DOMESDAY BOOK (1086) Shaftesbury and its abbey appear on various pages, usually including spellings of the modern name, or a reference to the abbey's dedication to St Mary. But in two instances the terse heading *Terra Sancti Edwardi*, 'Land of St Edward', stands in for the tongue-twisting *Sceptesberiensis*. And writing some forty years later during the 1120s the historian William of Malmesbury records that Shaftesbury was commonly known as 'St Edward's'. Latin forms of 'town of St Edward' or 'borough of St Edward' crop up in medieval documents, especially of the twelfth and thirteenth centuries, and the Saxon name *Edwardstow*, 'the place [or holy place] of Edward', is also found. In modern Shaftesbury this name is perpetuated in that of the town's only surviving medieval house, near the western end of Bimport. For a time in the early middle ages it seemed possible that Shaftesbury would follow the examples of *Medehampstead* (Peterborough), *Beadoriceswyrthe* (Bury St Edmunds), *Chich* (St Osyth) and *Twyneham* (Christchurch) – among others – and rename itself to honour the cult venerated in its abbey church. This chapter, a web of treachery, religion, politics and real estate, will be devoted to St Edward.[1]

Edward became king of England after his father, King Edgar, died in July 975. He was then about thirteen years old. He was the eldest of the dead king's three surviving children, the others being Edith and Aethelred. It is likely that all three had different mothers; Aethelred's mother, Queen Aelfthryth, survived her husband. Aethelred was about seven years old when his father died. The young Edward was king for less than three years. On 18 March 978, while

29

visiting his stepmother Aelfthryth and half-brother Aethelred at Corfe 'Gap' on Purbeck (Corfe Castle had not yet been built) he was set upon and murdered. No-one was subsequently found guilty of his murder. Aethelred succeeded his half-brother as king and reigned until 1016.[2]

Edwardstow, a late medieval house in Bimport flanked by eighteenth-century cottages.

These bald genealogical data form our starting point. But before we bring sainthood and Shaftesbury into the story we need to cast a critical eye over the evidence pertaining to the murder. We must also try to understand the political background to and significance of such an act.

When a king dies leaving two young children as his heirs it is inevitable that the kingly power must for a time be devolved elsewhere. Edward was Edgar's older son, but – unlike Aethelred – he had not been born during his father's reign as king. Consequently both had legitimate claims to the throne. The late Saxon kings of England ruled over an uneasy coalition of formerly autonomous states – Wessex, Mercia, Northumbria, etc – and their authority was forged through dynastic marriages and power-sharing arrangements with leading families and churchmen. Tensions during Edgar's reign, particularly between Archbishop Dunstan and Queen Aelfthryth, whose marriage the church regarded as improper, became focussed on the rival sons after his death. To some extent the polarisation into two camps can be assessed – Mercia on one side, East Anglia and Essex on the other – and it was clearly incumbent on Edward and his supporters to call in favours and make concessions to their opponents (by awarding them key appointments, for example) if conflict was to be avoided. Edward's murder signalled that they had failed.[3]

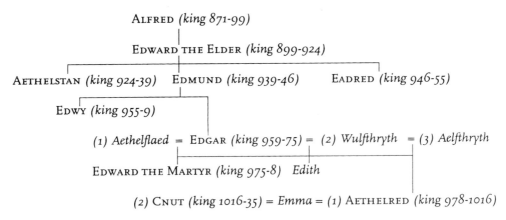

Simplified genealogical table showing Edward's place among the English kings from Alfred to Cnut.

Three near-contemporary accounts of the crime survive, as well as a *Passio*, or description of the saint's suffering, which was compiled somewhat later from a variety of oral and written sources. The earliest versions of the *Anglo-Saxon Chronicle*, probably written between 1016 and 1023, record the date of the murder at Corfe, in the evening, adding that the king was buried at Wareham with no royal honours. This is followed by a poem of lament, and against the following year is the information that the *eaolderman* Aelfhere took the body from Wareham and conveyed it with great ceremony to Shaftesbury. A rather different tradition is recorded in an influential sermon preached in 1014 by Wulfstan, archbishop of York, where as an example of disloyalty he singles out the murder: 'Edward was betrayed and then killed, and afterwards burnt.'[4]

The earliest account occurs in a life of St Oswald, which was probably written by an East Anglian monk, Byrhtferth, around 1000. He opens with a contrast between the happy reign of Edgar and the 'shipwreck' of state which raged after his death. This was exacerbated by the young Edward's violent temper, which was feared by everyone around him, and led his brother's ministers to plot against him. On a visit to his brother Aethelred and stepmother Aelfthryth, Edward was greeted by a cup-bearer, accompanied by a body of armed men who surrounded him, outnumbering his own bodyguard. One of the soldiers took him by the right hand as if to kiss him, while another grabbed his left hand and hurt him. Edward shouted, 'What are you doing, breaking my arm?' He suddenly jumped from his horse and was killed. The body was taken to a mean dwelling and hidden there, and later buried without due honour. Six months later the eaolderman Aelfhere exhumed the body, which he found intact and not decomposed; he cleaned and shrouded it, and removed it to another place for more honourable burial, where masses for the redemption of Edward's soul were celebrated.[5]

The fourth source, the *Passio et miracula sancti Eadwardi Regis et Martyris*, 'Suffering and miracles of St Edward King and Martyr', tells us by its title that it is not a work of history, but falls into the category known as hagiography, writings about saints. Such literature, widespread and popular in the middle ages, was designed to glorify God and his saints, to impress upon worshippers the virtues of the Christian life, and to help the pilgrim and supplicant in his or her veneration of a saint's relics. Hagiographical writing has similarities to folktales, with stock characters, miracles and wonders, and stereotypical formulae. The *Passio* of St Edward was probably written during the 1070s by Goscelin, a hagiographer who also wrote a life of St Edith of Wilton, Edward's half-sister, and who drew on materials – written sources and oral folktales – current at Shaftesbury Abbey. Of the murder itself he (or his source) embroiders some of the details after a story-teller's fashion: the wicked stepmother Aelfthryth contrives the murder; the Judas kiss is followed by a stab with a knife; the body is concealed in marshy ground and revealed by a wondrous column of fire; God appears in a vision to a blind woman living nearby; Aethelred is contrite with grief at his brother's death. Later much space is devoted to the body's translation to Shaftesbury and the miracles that occurred there.[6]

Standing back from these accounts, which were all written with the hindsight that the murdered king would subsequently be venerated as a saint, and which were all intended to convey a theological or political message, we may draw some tentative conclusions. Edward, after a short reign of turmoil and in-fighting, fell victim to a conspiracy hatched by his political opponents, who murdered him and disposed of his body, perhaps by burning it. Because the circumstances of his death (virtually on her doorstep during a social visit) were awkward to Aelfthryth and her protegé, the child-king Aethelred who succeeded to the throne, it was essential for her to distance herself from the murder. This she did, after considerable prevarication, by sending the eaolderman Aelfhere of Mercia, her close political ally and a man quite likely to have been implicated in the murder, to 'discover' the body of Edward and exalt it to a position of honour. Accordingly he went to Wareham, the nearest town to the scene of the crime, was given a fresh corpse (which he may or may not have believed to have been the undecayed body of Edward), and carried it in pomp to Shaftesbury Abbey.[7]

Aelfthryth, Aethelred and their supporters were in a delicate position. 'Kings are by God anointed', and so regicide amounted not only to murder but also to sacrilege. The murdered or sacrificed king was also a powerful folklore motif in pagan belief. So heinous a crime must be avenged, or at least appear to be avenged. But this was politically difficult, since the duty of vengeance fell on the deceased's family – his brother and stepmother – who were the very ones who had benefited from the murder, and whose supporters were most likely to have been the murderers. A new and fragile reign did not begin by placing its kingmakers on trial. More than a year elapsed after Edward's death before the coronation of Aethelred took place (in May 979), and during this interregnum a start had to be made on resolving the dilemma and deflecting guilt away from the new regime. Hence Aelfhere's mission to Wareham to find and exalt Edward's remains.[8]

There were precedents for avenging a royal murder. When one seventh-century Northumbrian king killed another, to whom he was related by marriage, he atoned for his crime by founding the monastery at Gilling, where his victim was buried and venerated as a saint. By the time of Edward's death a number of murdered kings and princes were regarded as martyrs and saints, and a hagiographical tradition had grown up about them which often included the foundation or endowment of monasteries where they could be venerated. The monasteries at Peterborough, Hereford and Minster-in-Thanet all

benefited in this way. It was a means of recompensing the church for the death
of its anointed without shedding any more royal blood; and the victim, however
unsaintly on earth, was granted his reward in heaven. Shaftesbury was the
foremost royal monastery in the shire of Edward's murder, and the resting-place
of his grandmother, Aelfgifu, who since her death in 944 was being venerated
as a saint. It was entirely appropriate, therefore, that the dead king's body be
brought to Shaftesbury for honourable burial, in a tomb near the principal altar
of the abbey church.[9]

Edward's passage from victim to martyr to saint was a rapid one. If we are
to believe Byrhtferth's account, written not much later than 1000, Edward's soul
spent five years after his arrival at Shaftesbury in Paradise, and after a further
six years miracles began to occur at his tomb, which were attested by many
people, including the archbishop of Canterbury. This would take us to about
990. In the years up to 1001 the *Passio* speaks of so very many miracles being
performed at his tomb that they were not even written down. Then in June 1001
the relics were moved from their tomb into the sanctuary of the abbey church.
Later in the same year, fearing that his brother's remains were under threat
from Viking marauders, Aethelred granted the Shaftesbury nuns the valuable
estate of Bradford on Avon, in north-west Wiltshire, where they were to
maintain a cell of the abbey and, if necessary, take Edward's and other relics for
safe keeping.[10]

There has been a great deal of scholarly discussion in recent years about
the political motivation of those who promoted the cult of St Edward during the
troubled years of Aethelred's reign. There is a view that his relics became the
rallying-point for those who opposed the government, who held Aelfthryth
responsible for the murder, and who saw the scourge of the Viking invasions as
God's punishment for this act of outrage. But the notion of the wicked
stepmother and the incompetent son (Aethelred, one recalls, has come down
through history as 'unready' or 'ill-advised'), bungling away the kingdom they
so dubiously inherited, is perhaps too facile. A contrary argument runs that they
were concerned to be seen to promote Edward's cult, so that it could not become
a focus of disaffection against them, or so that he and other saints would
intercede with God on their behalf against the Viking threat. It has been
suggested that the years between about 993–1006, despite Viking harassment,

was actually a period of stable government, when the king enjoyed good relations with the church, promoting monasteries and endowing churches. It seems to have been around then that the cult of Edward, and of his half-sister St Edith of Wilton, began with royal patronage to flourish. Was it not to Aethelred's advantage to promote his immediate family to the highest rank of all, sainthood, and thereby to imply that the royal family, including himself, was sacrosanct? It was certainly not in his interests to allow Edward's murder to set a precedent.[11]

Divine favour is a powerful weapon in tumultuous times. It might be enjoyed by the king to advantage, but only if it has been dispensed to him by God's agents on earth, the church. The relics of a fledgling royal saint performing miracles in Shaftesbury could be regarded as an asset to the king, or to his opponents, but they were a far greater asset to the nunnery. It was in the abbey's interest to develop the cult of St Edward by recording, publicising, and (a cynic might say) stage-managing miracles at his tomb, not only for commercial ends, but also as a means of wielding influence over the king, his half-brother. The 1001 ceremony of translating the relics into the sanctuary was doubtless intended to enhance St Edward's status, and it is perhaps no coincidence that a few months later, when a Viking raid seemed imminent, the abbess pressed home her advantage. 'Very probably', one historian has written, 'the nuns had tactfully pointed out to the ruler that it might prove embarrassing if the relics of his brother were to be destroyed by the Danes and that the problem might be solved by an extension of the abbey's landowning rights to include the *coenobium* [monastic cell] of Bradford on Avon.' Thus, by dint of its custody of some significant bones, Shaftesbury Abbey bargained for and acquired one

St Lawrence's chapel, Bradford on Avon, built perhaps to house St Edward's relics.

of its most valuable estates. The same historian goes on to suggest that the whole idea of St Edward the Martyr may have been invented by the nuns and sold, 'attractively packaged', to the king.[12]

After 1001 Edward's cult was promoted nationally in various ways. His relics seem never to have made the journey to Bradford on Avon, and body parts attributed to him remained at Shaftesbury throughout the middle ages, as the abbey's principal object of veneration and pilgrimage. In 1008 a secular law decreed that his mass day each March be observed throughout England. As a result his name and mass day occur in religious calendars and service books of the eleventh and later centuries from various places. Under Cnut, Aethelred's successor, Edward's bones were dispersed as relics to other monasteries, including Leominster and Abingdon; in the middle ages Exeter, Reading, Salisbury, St Albans, York and Durham all possessed a share, and Abingdon claimed to have 'the larger part' (*pars plurima*). How much stayed at Shaftesbury is not clear, but when the historian William of Malmesbury wrote about the abbey in the 1120s he commented tersely: 'Here also lies, or rather lay, St Edward. . .' – a remark which has been taken to mean that no bones remained.[13]

What impressed William was not Edward's bones, but his lung, which apparently was displayed still alive and breathing. If any credence is to be given to such a story at all, it is likely that what William saw, or was told about, were human viscera or internal organs kept in preserving fluid in a glass reliquary, for which parallels are known elsewhere. Remarkably, such a glass jar was discovered during the 1902–4 excavation campaign under a heart-shaped slab in front of the high altar. When found it had, apparently, contained a small shrivelled object like a pebble, which the excavator thought was the heart of Cnut. No-one at the time seems to have linked the 'pebble' with William's description of the preserved lung of St Edward, although the find-spot (if reported correctly) implies a relic of profound veneration. Cnut died at Shaftesbury in 1035, as we have seen, but was buried at Winchester, and there is no historical evidence that his heart remained in the abbey. The glass jar followed him to Winchester Cathedral in 1951 and subsequent expert analysis agreed that it was most probably a late-Saxon reliquary. The 'pebble' meanwhile had been lost, and its existence is only known from oral testimony current in 1959.[14]

The casket discovered by Claridge in 1931 after the removal of its contents.

The shrine of St Edward continued to be visited and venerated by pilgrims throughout the middle ages, and its significance in the life of the abbey and the town are referred to again in later chapters. But after the dissolution relics and the veneration of saints played no part in the reformed English church, and it might be expected that St Edward King and Martyr would have left Shaftesbury for ever along with the nuns whose guest he had been for so long. But on Thursday 22 January 1931 he came back! Or rather, a discovery was made which suggested that he had stayed on at the abbey site ever since the dissolution. John Wilson Claridge, son of the then recent purchaser of the abbey site, was engaged in clearing and digging out a corner of the north transept with his gardener, Bert Richards, when they came across a lead casket concealed beneath a large stone. Inside were human bones. The winter afternoon light was failing, so they stopped work. Friday was wet, but on Saturday Claridge (a professional actor) assembled the rector, the town clerk, his parents and three newspaper reporters to witness the excavation of his dramatic discovery. The base of the casket was too corroded for it to be lifted intact, so he removed its contents – part of a skull and bones amounting to about half the skeleton of a young man. Claridge was in no doubt that he had found the relics of St Edward, hastily secreted by the nuns at the dissolution of the abbey in a makeshift container. His find was reported in *The Times*, and briefly hit world headlines; it was referred to as, 'one of the greatest historical discoveries of the century'.[15]

When the fuss died down Claridge built a shrine for the bones and they remained on the abbey site until it was sold in 1951. He left Shaftesbury and

The reconsecration of the supposed bones of St Edward the Martyr at the abbey ruins in 1931.

took the bones with him in a leather bag. During the 1960s he struck up a friendship with an osteologist, Dr Stowell, who examined the bones and published a paper in 1970 which claimed that the evidence of injuries and age at death was consistent, to a remarkable degree, with the earliest detailed account of Edward's murder. A second examination in 1973–4, by the leading authority on bones from archaeological excavations, Dr Don Brothwell of the British Museum (Natural History), cast doubt on Stowell's interpretation. It was never published, but is believed to have shown that the bone fractures had occurred after death, and that the individual was of mature age and so could not have been the teenage Edward.[16]

Soon afterwards Claridge settled in Malta, but left the bones in a bank vault in England and made approaches to various ecclesiastics, including Shaftesbury's catholic priest, about a suitable home for them. None would accept them on the terms upon which Claridge insisted, 'that the relics should be enshrined and made available for prayer and reverence'. But in 1980 a member of the Russian Orthodox Church in Exile approached him, and was prepared not only to treat the bones with the reverence to which Claridge felt they were entitled, but even to purchase and adapt a former Anglican cemetery chapel, at Brookwood near Woking in Surrey, for their enshrinement. Agreement was reached and the work was completed in preparation for the enshrinement ceremony in September 1984. Russian Orthodox dignitaries from around the world made their way to Woking.[17]

At the eleventh hour John Wilson Claridge's elder brother, Geoffrey Claridge, a retired antiques dealer (both brothers by now were in their eighties), obtained a court injunction against the enshrinement. Geoffrey claimed that, as joint heir to their mother's estate, he was part owner of the bones, and he wished them to be returned to Shaftesbury. The high court judge dismissed the claim, but expressed dissatisfaction at the security arrangements in place to prevent the bones being stolen from their proposed shrine, and ordered them to stay where they were, in an old cutlery box in a vault in the Midland Bank, Woking. The enshrinement took place but was a somewhat muted affair, since after the ceremony the bones were taken back to the bank vault.[18]

The shrine built by Claridge to house St Edward's relics, and beyond it the crypt near where they were discovered.

Needless to say, this dramatic turn of events captured the attention of the national press, and the row continued intermittently for over four years.

Geoffrey Claridge died in 1986, but opposition to the enshrinement was continued by his daughter. In April 1988 the Attorney General stipulated the specific requirements for security at Brookwood and, when these were in place, the bones were permitted to be enshrined there in December 1988. John Wilson Claridge died in 1993, and his late brother's case against him was dismissed in 1995, to the dismay of those who wanted them returned to Shaftesbury. So at Brookwood the bones remain, and a special service was held in March 2001 to celebrate the millennium of their 1001 translation into the sanctuary of Shaftesbury Abbey.[19]

This chapter began with a dispute between two brothers and their supporters over their rightful inheritance, and with uncertainty over a murder and the murdered man's remains. It has ended, a thousand years later, in much the same way.

4 The Glory and the Ornament of the Town

But as Pythagoras did guesse at the vastnesse of Hercules' stature by the length of his foote, so among these Ruines are Remaynes enough left for a man to give a guesse what noble buildings, &c, were made by the Piety, Charity, and Magnanimity of our Forefathers.

JOHN AUBREY'S REMARK, made in the 1660s about antiquities in general, may very well be applied to Shaftesbury Abbey; for here, like Pythagoras, we have only footings and fragments from which to extrapolate the Herculean structure. To blame for the difficulty, in Aubrey's view, were 'the teeth of time and (which is more dangerous) the hands of mistaken zeale'. The effect of these two old enemies on Shaftesbury Abbey will be the subject of chapter 9. For the present we shall use the archaeological and historical evidence that remains to conjure up its medieval appearance.[1]

Within the abbey's precinct there were the religious buildings devoted to the worship of God, and the domestic buildings where the nuns and other convent members lived out their days and nights. There were also the functional buildings for the labour force, whose jobs were to serve the community's everyday needs, administer its estates and handle its dealings with the town and the outside world. Far and away the most striking of all these buildings to the medieval visitor was the abbey church – 'the glory and the ornament of the town', as Dorset's county historian described it.[2]

The ruins of the abbey church, looking eastward from the nave.

From the plan of the abbey church, excavated intermittently through the nineteenth and twentieth centuries and now exposed, and from the architectural fragments thereby recovered, it is clear that a total rebuilding of the church began towards the end of the eleventh century and continued early into the twelfth, so from about 1080–1120. This work is presumed to have begun (as was the usual fashion) at the east end – the sanctuary – and continued steadily westwards, to the quire, the transepts and lastly the nave. There is a

The chancel, looking south-east, with area of exposed tiles in the foreground.

tradition that the east end was consecrated by Archbishop Anselm which, if true, would point to completion of this part in about 1108. The style was heavy Norman Romanesque, with round-headed arches, including arcades of cylindrical columns dividing the nave from its aisles, and a squat central tower. The east end was apsidal (semi-circular) with flanking apsidal chapels to north and south, although these were square-ended externally. Both transepts also had apsidal east chapels, but they were later obscured by rebuilding. There were chapels, too, in the nave aisles, and a screen (or pulpitum) across the nave near its eastern end to divide the nave from the crossing and quire. Local greensand was the dominant material, but some of the fine facing stone for the new building came from quarries on the abbey's estate of Tisbury.[3]

Model, by Laura Sydenham, of the abbey church, cloisters and chapter house, on display in the museum (above). The model is based on archaeological evidence, architectural fragments, and the design of the abbey seal (right). Many details are conjectural, but overall the model gives a good impression of how Shaftesbury Abbey may have appeared after the Norman rebuilding.

Although this church has been lost we can envisage it from the reconstruction painting and model in the abbey museum, and we are probably familiar with similar buildings – the larger churches, cathedrals and abbeys of Norman England – which have survived. Because the survivors are quite numerous and widespread we are apt to take them for granted, without considering what a revolution was taking place to create them. This great rebuilding between about 1050 and 1150 of churches everywhere, importing ideas, designs and techniques from continental Europe, has been described as, 'a movement of almost seismic character, involving the commitment of craftsmen and resources on an unprecedented scale'. In its local Wessex context the work at Shaftesbury began earlier than most of the larger church-rebuilding projects, such as Wimborne Minster and Sherborne Abbey in Dorset, Malmesbury Abbey in Wiltshire, or Romsey Abbey in Hampshire. Its closest architectural parallel is the near-contemporary Old Sarum cathedral, which was begun in 1075 and consecrated in 1092. Like Shaftesbury it too exists now only as a two-dimensional ground plan, rather than as a three-dimensional church, but in the original design (it was altered a few decades later) its arrangement of apses at the east end and transepts with apsidal chapels was very similar. The cathedral's dimensions, however, were slightly smaller than Shaftesbury, so it is quite likely that the abbey church was the largest and most ambitious building project of its generation undertaken in the diocese.[4]

To plan, fund and build a church to rival – even outstrip – the cathedral of its diocese suggest a powerful personality in charge. Shaftesbury was still favoured by the aristocracy, and to some extent by the Norman royal house, but it was no longer under royal patronage as in the days of Alfred or Aelfthryth. The driving force was not therefore the Crown, but was presumably the abbess. We know a little about Eulalia, whose dates seem to coincide with the rebuilding – she was elected abbess in 1074 and remained until her death around 1106. Her name suggests that she was a native of France, and she had a relative, Thomas, who was a tenant on abbey estates at Bradford, Atworth and Donhead. She succeeded Leofgifu, an Englishwoman, and so was the first Norman abbess of Shaftesbury. One hint of her strong character may come in Domesday Book, which states that King William had returned to the abbess the manors of Cheselbourne and Stour, wrongly taken from her by his predecessor. Another,

Reconstruction of the abbey church interior, looking east along the nave (painting by Ronald Homes displayed in the abbey museum).

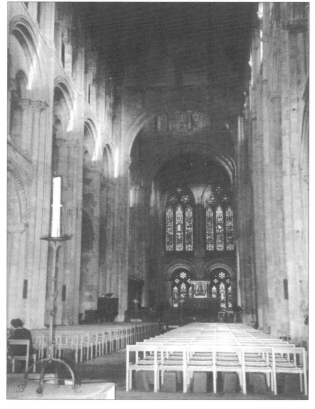

Romsey abbey church, Hampshire, offers a reasonably close architectural parallel to the lost church at Shaftesbury. These views show the exterior from the north-east (top), the nave (left) and the south chapel (above).

perhaps originating as a comment or joke on her impetuous nature, is found in a collection of miracles of the Virgin Mary – who appeared to her in a vision and asked her to say her *Ave Maria* more slowly! As an administrator it was presumably she who ordered to be drawn up the surviving list of lands allotted for military service, and perhaps also that of nuns' dowries, both of which appear to date from her reign. And as a propagandist she must have promoted the cult of St Edward, whose *Passio* was compiled by Goscelin at this time. In her lifetime she corresponded with Archbishop Anselm, who was clearly on very friendly terms with her, and after her death her memory continued to be respected by including her name on bede-rolls at the great Benedictine houses of Caen and Savigny in Normandy, whereby prayers would have been said for her soul.[5]

Anyone who enjoys visiting medieval churches will know that as much pleasure is to be derived from the appreciation of small details as from the overall impact of the grand design. At Shaftesbury the high quality

Carved stone fragments from the abbey.

and craftsmanship of the masons employed by Eulalia and her successors to build and decorate their church may still be seen in the fragments of window-glass, carved stonework and decorated tiles displayed in the abbey museum and (in the latter case) *in situ* among the ruins. The floor tiles in particular (of which more than 6,500 pieces survive, representing more than 100 designs) have been the subject of great interest and study. They date from the late-thirteenth and fourteenth centuries and must once have covered most of the church. Many bear heraldic or armorial designs, including those of local families, or stylised beasts such as lions, griffins and stags associated with heraldry. One floor depicted a hunting scene, and many tiles employed fashionable motifs of the day, such as the fleur-de-lys and the marguerite. A few tiles exhibit a most unusual technique of decoration, known as barbotine, achieved by squeezing the coloured slip through a nozzle before glazing and firing.[6]

In common with all living places of worship the medieval abbey church accumulated works of art, devotion and memorial throughout its existence, and some of these have been recovered by excavation and are on display. Far more has been lost, and the bright colours, gilding, incense and mystery can now only be recaptured in the imagination. Frank Hopton, whose study of the abbey buildings illuminates so much of its history, has described the scene:

> There were large wall spaces, plastered or lime-washed before being painted in bright colours with scenes from Bible stories – 'books for the people', as Pope Gregory the Great called them. Pilgrims and townspeople entering by the west door would have seen, first a large expanse of tiled floor, uncluttered by pews or stools, extending as far as the nave altar. Behind this focal point was the wooden rood screen, carved with pinnacles and canopied niches for statues of saints with gilded haloes and brightly coloured vestments of red and blue, green and yellow. Above the altar was the rood itself, a large impressive statue of Christ hanging on the cross. Within the side aisles and transepts were the chantry chapels, perhaps as many as ten by soon after 1400 when St Catherine's was founded. The nave altar and the chantry altars were centres of light and colour with their candles, crosses, embroidered altar cloths, both frontals and dorsals, their painted reredos and statues – in St Catherine's chapel with the gilded, coloured alabaster panels of the retable.[7]

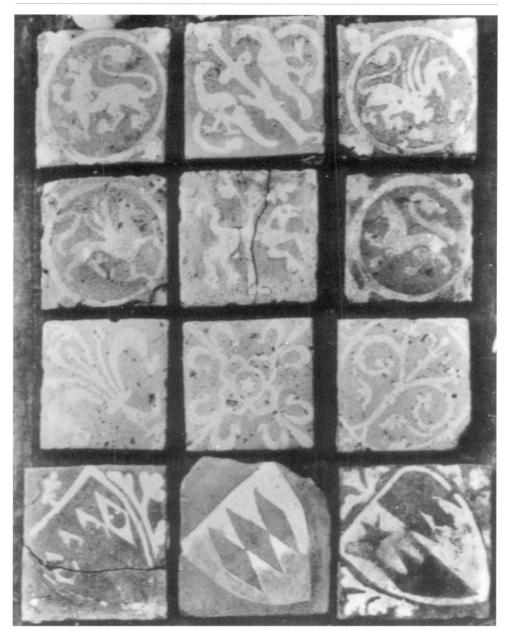

Examples of floor tiles recovered from the abbey church and chapter house.

But at Shaftesbury Abbey, unlike most equivalent architectural masterpieces, there was little attempt to improve, expand and rebuild the basic structure itself. The only significant alterations were made during the fourteenth century when the transept chapels were replaced, and the pulpitum and screens removed from the nave and a new pulpitum built east of the crossing. Opening from the north transept a new square-ended chapel was built with a crypt beneath, almost certainly to provide a shrine where visitors could venerate the remains of St Edward without disrupting the devotions of the nuns in the chancel. The counterpart of this new chapel on the south was a larger south chapel, probably intended as a Lady Chapel, which reflected the growing interest by the laity in the cult of Mary.[8]

The crypt beneath the chapel leading from the north transept.

It is possible to explain both the lack of substantial change to the church throughout its history, and the relatively modest fourteenth-century alterations, in terms of the number of nuns accommodated by the abbey. The pulpitum and screens across the nave near its eastern end demarcated the areas set aside for the nuns (to the east) and the laity (to the west). As the number of nuns grew to around 120 during the thirteenth century all the space in church allotted to them – the chancel, transepts, crossing and eastern bay of the nave – was needed. But when numbers fell during the fourteenth century they could retreat to the chancel alone, so that laity could be permitted access to the transepts and crossing, and therefrom to the new chapels of St Edward and Our Lady. The

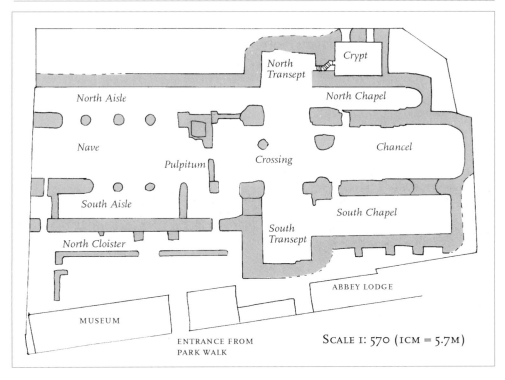

Simplified plan of the excavated portion of the abbey church (after Corney 2002).

superfluity of nuns during the thirteenth century presented not only the problem of accommodating them all in church, but also of sustaining them within the abbey's budget. Whereas numbers in male monasteries during this period were declining, nunneries were becoming ever more popular among aristocratic families as culs-de-sac for surplus female offspring, and even the wealthiest, including Shaftesbury and Wilton, found their incomes insufficient to meet their commitments. There was no money to spare on rebuilding the church. At Wilton repeated financial crises through the thirteenth century left the church and abbey buildings in disrepair. Shaftesbury, from the fourteenth century and earlier, according to one historian, 'was continuously crippled by insufficient means and its existence chequered by the constant recurrence of debt and insolvency'.[9]

Within the monastic precinct the abbey church was not the only place of worship. The present Holy Trinity church (though no longer in religious use) remains a dominant landmark on Shaftesbury's skyline and a focal presence

Holy Trinity church.

within the townscape. It was built between 1840 and 1842 but occupies the site of its medieval predecessor, which was likewise a substantial church with aisles and a west tower. Holy Trinity began as a chapel within the abbey graveyard (in the same way as St Paul's church, Malmesbury, whose tower remained to house the bells when the abbey tower collapsed), and it served as a place of worship for townspeople and perhaps abbey servants. In 1364 one of the most precious chantries in the abbey church, the altar of the Holy Rood, was transferred with its chaplain to Holy Trinity because of the disruption caused to the nuns by throngs of worshippers focussing their Maytime revels on it.[10]

Visitors to the ruins of the abbey church today will have entered from the south – Park Walk – and quite understandably may assume that this too was how their medieval predecessors arrived. In fact the abbey gatehouse stood in Bimport, to the north, astride the modern lane called Abbey Walk. It gave access to a large monastic precinct, whose bounds are represented today by Bimport on the north, Magdalene Lane on the west and Lyons Walk on the east. To the south the edge of the promontory made a natural boundary, and beyond it sloped away

Reconstruction, by Frank Garbutt, of the view of the abbey and promontory from the south.

the abbey park. From a medieval perspective the open area of the present Park Walk outside the abbey museum entrance was the quietest (weather permitting), most private and secluded part of the complex, and it was here that the convent buildings of the nuns, where they worked, met, slept, and ate, were grouped around a cloister.

Park Walk (apart from one small trench) has never been excavated, and the form of these buildings is little known. The north walk of the cloister, however, and parts of its east and west walks, lie open within the precinct of the ruins and beneath the museum and shop buildings. Assuming the usual monastic arrangement around a square cloister the approximate position of a

Fragments of the north walk of the cloister, looking south-west from the nave.

south range, occupied by the refectory and kitchen, can be estimated. Part of the lavishly tiled chapter house, which was separated from the south transept by a narrow passage (or slype), has been excavated; and upstairs, along the eastern range of the cloister, the dormitory must have run, since the foot of the connecting nightstairs may still be seen leading from it into the church. The abbess's lodging may have occupied or adjoined the western range of the cloister, but this is conjectural. Somewhere nearby should have been the infirmary (Abbey House further west may be on its site). All these buildings were demolished soon after the dissolution, so that by 1565 only fragments and parts of associated chambers remained.[11]

Away from the claustral buildings, which as any visitor to monastic sites will know tend to conform to a stereotype, we should be able to deduce very little about the position, layout and function of the rest of the monastic complex, were it not for three invaluable documents drawn up during the time of destruction. Two, of 1548 and 1574, are brief descriptions of the site included in a much wider-ranging survey of the landholdings of the earl of Pembroke. This survey, formerly at Wilton House, has been published, and the original document is now in the Wiltshire and Swindon Record Office. The third document is now lost, but it survived long enough for a transcript to be made and published in the eighteenth century. It is a detailed survey of all the abbey buildings as they survived or could be recognised in 1565, apparently made for

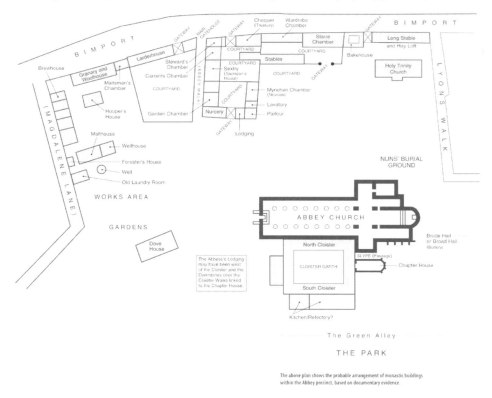

Plan of the abbey precinct, reconstructed by Frank Hopton.

the purpose of dividing the site into three roughly equal portions – a division which was never implemented. By a detailed analysis of these surveys, and comparison with the buildings and boundaries shown on maps of Shaftesbury of 1615 and 1799, Frank Hopton has been able to reconstruct a hypothetical ground plan of much of the precinct; this is displayed in the abbey museum.[12]

Most of the functional buildings lay close to the northern edge of the site, along Bimport. But there was one building, described as the Broad Hall, which overlooked, and perhaps dominated, the market place of the medieval town, rather as Lord Grosvenor's town hall has dominated it for much of the last two centuries. The site is now occupied by a restaurant, King Alfred's, and adjoining

Site of the Broad Hall, facing Shaftesbury's market place.

buildings running south from Church Lane. The Broad Hall included a chamber, cellar, wine cellar, pantry, buttery and almonry, from where doles of food and drink would have been dispensed to poor townspeople. It appears from the 1615 Shaftesbury map to have been a long building and, although we know nothing of its architecture or range of functions, it is perhaps to be compared with the inns and guesthouses built in town centres by monasteries during the later middle ages. Such buildings exist or existed in west-country towns, at Sherborne and Malmesbury, Glastonbury and Gloucester; the George Inn at Norton St Philip south of Bath is a spectacular survivor.[13]

King Edward's Court, on the site of the abbey courtyards.

Abbey buildings seem to have formed an almost continuous frontage along Bimport, from Lyons Walk to Magdalene Lane, with the exception of two entrances, a gateway leading to Holy Trinity and the abbey gatehouse on the site of the present Abbey Walk turning. Running south from the gatehouse and east along Bimport were buildings ranged around courtyards, and in these were conducted the business of the abbey estate. Here were the 'Star Chamber', most probably where the business of the manorial courts was conducted, and the 'Cheker', or exchequer, which handled financial matters. Here too were offices for the steward, a male official who was the chief executive of the monastic business, and for those senior nuns (known as obedientiaries) who held important posts within the hierarchy. They included the sacrist, who was responsible for all the equipment required for services in the church; the chambress, who looked after the wardrobe; and the mistress of the novices, whose living and learning accommodation was also here. Finally in this part of the campus were stables, a hayloft and a bakery.[14]

The more manual tasks, undertaken by abbey servants, took place to the west of the gatehouse in what was referred to as a base court, and which corresponds to the area between Abbey Walk and Magdalene Lane. Here were the storage and industrial units for grain and malt, the larder house for other foodstuffs, the well house and wool house, the hooper's workshop where barrels were made, stores for building materials, timber and lime, as well as wood to fuel the brewery furnace. A well to supply the water for brewing and food preparation also lay in this area, and it was rediscovered by archaeologists when the hospital car park was extended in 1996. Their excavation also discovered lime-kilns and a furnace, and traces of industrial buildings around a courtyard, thus confirming the deductions drawn from the sixteenth-century surveys. Remote from this main complex in the base court were further buildings, a pigeon house (roughly where the war memorial now stands) and a laundry. Presumably because it was easier to take the washing to the water supply than vice versa, this latter necessity lay beneath the promontory behind St James. The lane leading there down the hillside, now known as Stoney Path, was formerly called Launder Lane.[15]

The serene world of prayer and contemplation, the business world of tenancy agreements and expenses, and the menial world of cooking and laundry, were all co-existing within the abbey walls throughout the middle ages. But outside those walls were parallel worlds of devotion, business and housework, about which, unfortunately, we know very little. The town of Shaftesbury, as we saw in chapter 2, seems to have moved itself during the eleventh and twelfth centuries off the promontory and into the more spacious area south and east of the abbey, which it still occupies. Under the Norman and Plantagenet kings towns sprang up and grew, as the population nationally increased and more peaceful conditions prevailed than hitherto. By the time that this phase of urban expansion was ending, around 1300, Shaftesbury had attracted many incomers and traders; it was easily the wealthiest town in Dorset, and one of the wealthiest in the west country. Its progress thereafter, before and after the abbey's dissolution, will be the theme of chapter 8. But, having spent some time exploring within the precinct, we should perhaps glimpse what we can of the changes taking place outside.

It seems clear that between 1100 and 1300 Shaftesbury capitalized on its position at the meeting of traditional trade routes between London and the south-west, and between the south coast and Bristol region. It also had the advantage of lying at the interface of different geological and farming regions – chalk, greensand and clay. And it could reap the same benefits as other towns that adjoined major monasteries, from the visits of pilgrims, traders and administrators, and from the wealth created by the abbey. With all these trading

Shaftesbury's medieval market spaces, High Street and the Commons, seen from Gold Hill.

advantages it is easy to understand why open marketing areas developed between the top of Gold Hill and the area known as the Commons, extending eastwards along the present High Street (earlier known as Cornhill).

Like other towns making headway in a competitive landscape Shaftesbury was keen to safeguard its market. It is mentioned as a borough in 1244, and the first royal charter recognizing the town's borough status was obtained in 1252. The right to hold weekly markets and take a toll from traders was confirmed by the Crown in 1269, and Jewish moneylending was carried on before 1276. From 1295 it sent representatives to Parliament, and soon after a 'borough reeve' (a forerunner of the office of mayor) occurs in documents. There were property developers too. It is possible to detect in the layout of boundaries within the town blocks of regular burgage plots, and these are symptomatic of piecemeal urban development in the middle ages. Although very little modern systematic excavation has taken place within the medieval town, a site recently investigated between High Street and Bell Street discovered pits containing twelfth- and thirteenth-century pottery. It is to be hoped that the opportunity will be taken to examine any similar town-centre sites which may come up for redevelopment in future, so that Shaftesbury's medieval growth, alongside that of its abbey, can be better understood.[16]

5 Gentle Modesty, Gracious Austerity

ONTEMPLATING HER DEATH after 32 years as abbess Dame Joan Formage drew up a will in May 1394. She had already begun disposing of her possessions to various friends and good causes, and her will stipulated many similar bequests to take effect at the time of her death and burial, which occurred nearly three months later. During her long reign her abbey had seen good times and bad. There had been a rebuilding campaign during the 1360s which probably included the lengthening of the chapels on either side of the chancel. In 1381 there had been a financial crisis brought on by cattle plague on the abbey estates. If the dissension and unpleasantness surrounding the choice of her successor is any guide her later years may have been marred by factional quarrels among her nuns. Towards the end she was either losing her grip on the discipline of the house, or perhaps she no longer cared. The drunken parties in the infirmary, to which some of the nuns invited men, and the love letters – these were roundly condemned by the bishop in 1392. We shall return to them later. But Dame Joan may never have cared too much for the more rigorous aspects of the devotional life. In 1368 she had sought and received permission to leave her abbey and spend a year on one of

opposite: *Virgin and Child, from the Shaftesbury Psalter, c. 1130–50 (British Library Lansdowne MS 383, f.165v).*

her manors (probably Tisbury), 'for air and recreation'. The making of a will was in itself an act of defiance (her vow of poverty precluding her from owning possessions) and it was annulled by the bishop immediately after her death. He tried, perhaps in vain, to recover abbey property which she had already given away.[1]

Dame Joan's will, because it was the work of a maverick, stands apart from the generally terse and turgid references to Shaftesbury Abbey in the medieval national archives. It opens a window into the abbess's lodging, and illumines three aspects of life in the community. First it is written in the courtly French which persisted in nunneries as a mark of aristocratic breeding long after it had evaporated elsewhere. Second it catalogues the comforts and extravagances enjoyed by a woman of Joan's standing. And third, it tells us about hierarchies within and beyond the convent, the nuns, the novices, the men and the servants. This chapter will attempt to explore life within Shaftesbury Abbey from these three angles.

The medium, it might be said, is part of the message of Joan's will. Her use of French, rather than Latin or English, to phrase the universal beliefs of will-makers, gives the process a refined and gentle air: *ce qu'est pur la meillour salvacion de nostre alme* ('which is for the better salvation of our soul'). Norman French, both spoken and written, probably came to Shaftesbury Abbey with Eulalia, the first post-conquest abbess (1074–1106), and may have lingered here well into the fifteenth century. During the Norman period high-born Englishwomen (from whose ranks the nuns were recruited) thought and spoke in French, and some were sent to Normandy to complete their education. Their understanding of Latin, though sufficient to sing the liturgy in church, was probably not great, and nunneries never shared the tradition of Latin scholarship and manuscript copying of their male counterparts. By the fifteenth century French too was waning, and English had become the language of comprehension and conversation.[2]

The evidence for these generalized statements may be seen at Shaftesbury in the few books to have survived which were once possessed by the nuns. Shortly before 1300 a chaplain *del iglise seint edward* ('St Edward's church', i.e. Shaftesbury), William Giffard, produced a version of the Apocalypse (or Book of Revelations), with a commentary, in rather bad French

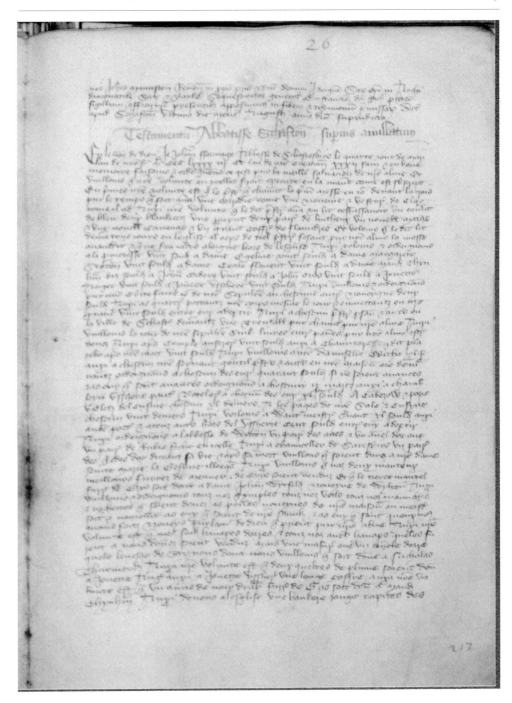

Part of the will of Joan Formage, 1394, copied into Bishop Waltham's register (WSRO D1/2/14, f.217r).

verse, and added for good measure an essay on the seven deadly sins. Giffard, as well as serving as chaplain, was also rector of Litton Cheney in Dorset from 1298–1302, and was undoubtedly a relative of Dame Mabel Giffard, the abbess from 1291 until 1302. His purpose in writing the book was to provide a confessional manual for the Shaftesbury nuns (he was perhaps their confessor), and he wrote in French verse specifically *bien eit ke les mettra ben en memoire*, 'so that it will be easier for them to memorize'.[3]

Six liturgical manuscript books have been associated with Shaftesbury Abbey, with varying degrees of confidence. One, a breviary (which would have contained the various offices of the daily worship), is referred to in Dame Joan's will – it had been acquired by one of her sister nuns, Margaret Stourton. Three others are illuminated psalters, containing the Psalms in Latin, together with various prayers, creeds, litanies and calendars. Another, the well-known 'Winchester Psalter', with 38 full pages of illumination, is written in Latin and French. Although produced at Winchester in the mid-twelfth century this most beautiful of books soon thereafter passed to Shaftesbury and must have been one of the community's most treasured possessions. Finally in this group is a book of hours, the sequence of eight devotions known as the little office of the Virgin Mary, which were modelled on the daily round of monastic services. The book contains additional prayers, psalms and verses, as well as information about its origins and history. It was made for Dame Elizabeth Shelford, who was abbess 1505–28; it then passed to the rector of St Rumbold's, Cann, in the Shaftesbury suburbs; and just before the dissolution it returned to the abbey in the possession of a nun, Alice Champnys – she had bought it from the rector for ten shillings.[4]

Besides these books, intended for liturgical and private prayer, and so written in Latin, there have survived in two collections an assortment of devotional works in English, including *The Ladder of Perfection*, *The Rule of Life of Our Lady*, *The Pater Noster of Richard the Hermit*, and many titles in a similar vein. Both collections belonged to the abbey during the fifteenth century, one the gift of a benefactor, the other the possession of a nun.[5]

Though the books that survive can be but a small sample of the contents of the abbey library, they do reflect the community's use of three languages: Latin for worship, French and later English for day-to-day life. And there is one further pointer, unfortunately rather speculative, to the level of cultural attainment nurtured within the abbey. The first woman writer in French is known only as Marie de France. She was a poet, who wrote versions of Aesop's *Fables* and verse romances on chivalric and folktale themes known as *Lais*. Apart from her name, and other deductions which can be made from allusions in her work – her aristocratic connections, her Breton origins, her knowledge of and residence in England or Wales, and a date of writing in the second half of the twelfth century – nothing is known about her. In 1910 a Norman-French scholar, Sir John Fox, put forward arguments to identify her with Marie, illegitimate half-sister of Henry II, and abbess of Shaftesbury between 1181 and 1216. If he were right then the abbey, where presumably much of her work would have been written, could make the extraordinary claim to be one of the cradles of French literature. Without fresh evidence the issue may never be resolved, and while few writers on Marie since 1910 have accepted Fox's identification unreservedly, the abbess continues to be taken seriously as one of several possible contenders. The important point is perhaps that there is nothing incongruous about a twelfth-century Shaftesbury abbess being identified with an author who, in her native French, spun exquisite tales of love and treachery, foundlings and adulterers, villainy, lust and murder.[6]

We have moved far from the monastic stereotype, and before leaving the subject of literature we should cast another glance at Dame Shelford's book of hours. The traditional Latin text of the little office, contained therein, was recited as a form of private devotion. Alice Champnys, its purchaser, followed her inscription of ownership with a prayer, in English, which will serve to remind us that the essence of being a nun was communion with God:

> O swete Jhesu, the sonne of God, the endles swetnesse of hevyn and of erthe and of all the worlde, be in my herte, in my mynde, in my wytt, in my wylle, now and ever more, Amen. Jhesu mercy, Jhesu gramercy [*grand merci*, 'great thanks'], Jhesu for thy mercy, Jhesu as I trust to thy mercy, Jhesu as thou art fulle of mercy, Jhesu have mercy on me and alle mankynd redemyd with thy precyouse blode.[7]

This expression of Christian faith, penned in the final years of the community's existence, may be paralleled by another, written more than four centuries earlier, as the rebuilt Norman abbey was nearing completion. It comes in one of three letters sent to the abbess Eulalia and her nuns by Anselm, archbishop of Canterbury. After three years in exile Anselm returned to England in 1106 and wrote to Shaftesbury to thank the nuns for their prayers during his absence. He offered them this advice:

> Your community ought to be a temple of God and the temple of God is holy. If therefore you live in a holy manner, as I hope you do, then you are the temple of God. You live in a holy manner if you diligently keep your rule and your intention. You do this diligently if you do not scorn the smallest things. . . As it is true that one who despises little things fails little by little so it is true that one who does not despise little things progresses little by little.[8]

For every nun, pious or wayward, the daily round of religious services (the offices ordained in the Benedictine rule) punctuated by interludes of work, reading, meals and sleep, became second nature. Like breathing, it was continuous and unremitting, requiring no record and no remark unless interrupted. At Shaftesbury recorded interruptions were rare – townspeople larking about and swearing noisily in the churchyard to the disruption of services were censured by the bishop in 1311. In 1367, as we have seen, the holiday crowd attending early at the altar of Holy Cross in the abbey church disturbed the nuns' rest after the labours of the night and their devotions. But in general, like a wheel endlessly turning, we must assume from the silence in the sources that the work of the nunnery went on unhindered.[9]

In a world which set the highest premium on the efficacy of prayer, monastic houses were factories – power stations almost – where prayer was generated. This can be gauged by the fervour with which wealthy families bought into this power source by endowing chantry chapels and altars in and around the abbey church. Thomas Platel, for example, who represented Shaftesbury in Parliament between 1338 and 1344, earmarked

Nuns at their devotions, a drawing by Frank Garbutt.

rent from property in the town (Platel's market) for a chantry priest, to celebrate daily for ever, for the good estate of himself and his wife Alice, and for their souls after their decease; and for the souls of Thomas and Agnes, parents of his first wife Christian, and their ancestors, heirs and benefactors. This was in 1342. The prayers continued for 120 years, and a succession of 22 priests who daily prayed them has been recorded.[10]

The nave aisles in the fourteenth and fifteenth centuries filled up with these mysterious memorials to dead benefactors, and a background buzz of

Nuns emerging from the nightstair, a drawing by Frank Garbutt.

mumbled praying must have greeted the ears of visitors. The saints they venerated, and some of the families they commemorated, are known, while the memory of others has been lost. Several were founded by abbesses, including a very rich endowment made by Dame Margaret St John in 1492 for a chaplain to pray at the Lady Chapel altar. Margaret was the aunt of the king, Henry VII, and prayers were to be said for members of the Tudor dynasty, including Henry's parents and queen, Elizabeth, the mother of Henry VIII. The endowment, when it was finally authorized in 1498, included an impressive portfolio of land, comprising seven houses, three dovecotes and over 500 acres of land in the Shaftesbury area of north Dorset, together with four houses and nearly 300 acres of land in neighbouring parts of Wiltshire. Sixty years later, when the chantry was suppressed (by a descendant of the family commemorated) the chaplain was responsible not only for the prayers, but also for giving alms to the poor every Friday, and for administering the estate. His 1553 account showed a healthy profit of income over expenditure (principally his salary).[11]

Dame Joan Formage, in her will which began this chapter, did not go to such lengths to secure her eternal salvation. She did, however, bequeath sums of money to five sister nunneries in Wessex to pray for her soul, and made elaborate and expensive arrangements for the prayers to be said at her funeral. She also provided the first mass priest of the day with a corrody or pension in return for his daily prayers on her behalf, as well as a bed, bedding and other comfortable furnishings within the church, presumably to mitigate the unsocial hours he had to spend there.[12]

Indeed comfort (luxury even) rather than monastic austerity, seems to have been a characteristic of Joan's lifestyle. She had three coats lined with fur, two furred in grey, one in white (miniver), and a black cloth hood furred in grey. Her silver plates, dishes and saucers she left to St Edward's shrine along with a gold brooch. Her rings, including a golden ring set with a ruby, she bequeathed to the abbess of Wilton. Her five golden goblets were to be sold, along with her other goblets, but a cup with a golden lid (a present from the bishop) was to go to a male relative, Nicholas Thurmond. Her furniture included a red bench embroidered with a design of birds and leaves, and with ten red cushions.[13]

Evidence about life in a specific monastery can be divided into two categories. There are passing references to the humdrum, and there are occasional crises and scandals. Joan Formage's will falls into the latter category, and we know its contents only because a higher authority (the bishop) disapproved of it. But that does not necessarily mean that it gives a misleading picture of normal monastic life. 'Scandals' occur when opinions clash about acceptable behaviour. Over-zealous bishops or over-decadent nuns?   The historian must attempt to achieve a balance.

Nuns, as we have seen, were recruited from the upper echelons of society, from aristocratic and wealthy families who for economic or dynastic reasons decided to pay their dowry to a nunnery rather than see their daughter married. Girls might enter a nunnery at a very young age. Agnes de la Ryver took the veil at Shaftesbury aged seven, and about nine years later, in 1374, professed her vows as a regular nun. She remained in her vows throughout her life. Bartholomia Raynold, on the other hand, entered the nunnery from her home in Melcombe Regis (Weymouth) when she was ten in about 1520. Before she professed her vows at the age of nineteen she visited her parents for their blessing, and confided that she would rather spend £40 than go back to the nunnery. But the abbey servants came to fetch her, and she remained at

Shaftesbury as a nun until about two years before the dissolution. Unfortunately for her she had gone by the time that the pensions were handed out![14]

From such beginnings it is clear that some nuns, like Agnes, accepted their lot. There were opportunities for promotion to positions of importance and authority (rare for women in medieval England), such as one of the obedientiaries (sacrist, chambress, or mistress of the novices), the sub-prioress, prioress or even abbess. Of fifteen abbesses between 1216 and 1377, eight were drawn from Shaftesbury nuns, two had been sub-prioress and four prioress.

The abbess and the novice, a drawing by Frank Garbutt.

Only one had come from elsewhere: Agnes Longespee in 1246 transferred from Wherwell, where she had been a nun. Conversely Katherine Moleyns, a Shaftesbury nun, was appointed prioress of the small nunnery at Kington St Michael in Wiltshire in 1492. As Shaftesbury's abbess a woman had reached pre-eminence in society. She could stand up to bullying royal officials and win, as in a long-standing argument over whether she should pay to mend a bridge at Old Sarum castle. In similar robust fashion she successfully defended the abbey's right to collect firewood daily from Gillingham Forest. Her status entitled her to the rank of baron, though women never sat in Parliament. She also played hostess to members of royal families, such as Elizabeth de Burgh, queen of Robert the Bruce of Scotland, who was held at Shaftesbury under virtual house arrest in 1312–14; or Catherine of Aragon, future wife of Henry VIII, in 1501. She was the mistress of vast estates.[15]

But even the might of the abbess of Shaftesbury could not prevail over the misogynist bias of medieval theology. Because a nunnery was composed of women, canon law required that it be supervised by the bishop of its diocese, who had the power to reprimand under threat of excommunication any nun of whose behaviour he disapproved. At the time of Joan Formage's death in 1394 he went further, and tried to influence the outcome of the nuns' election of a successor. 'Since women's ill-advised frailty needed the more informed guidance of men', he sent in three male clergy as commissioners to hold discussions with the prioress and convent before the election, 'to instruct them to act scrupulously in good conscience and freely elect an abbess able to rule to the praise of God and the observance of the religious life'.[16]

The assumption underlying such a view was not only that women were inferior, but also that their 'frailty' made them more susceptible to sins of the flesh. As such they were a moral danger to themselves and to any men whom they might lead astray. The church therefore tried to enforce on nuns strict enclosure within their precincts, making their convent their prison. For those nuns who, channelled into the religious life before puberty and against their will, felt no sense of vocation, this might seem an intolerable affront to their liberty and their femininity. It is hardly surprising that they rebelled.[17]

In 1309 Bishop Simon of Ghent wrote to the abbess following a recent inspection of the abbey. He had been particularly dismayed by the conduct of a nun, Christine Baryl, and absolutely forbade her from being permitted to leave. As for the other nuns, if they had any cause to go out, for health reasons, water or air, they must seek permission, and must not be allowed to enter houses in Shaftesbury town or elsewhere, even those of priests and persons of rank, unless chaperoned. Bishop Hallum, two centuries later, tried to enforce the same restriction. He had heard that nuns and sisters, with their superior's permission, often spent the day going out to various places in brightly coloured clothes. He reminded them of the Old Testament story of Dinah, who went out on pleasure bent and was seduced by a neighbouring prince (they may have already considered this), and warned them not to unlock the gates of their senses and let in the wicked spirit.[18]

One other letter, from Bishop Waltham in 1392, during the closing years of Joan Formage's reign, suggests that the nuns were then enjoying a social life more reminiscent of St Trinian's than St Edward's:

> The Vicar General has heard that some influential nuns, very often intent upon bringing men into the infirmary, held feasts and drinking sessions resulting in drunkenness, and otherwise acted there contrary to the Rule. Others had amorous

letters which they sent to lovers and suspect persons, sealed with appropriate seals and signets.

The abbess was told to admonish them, and to confiscate their seals and signets.[19]

The wording of this letter suggests that under Joan there were tensions within the community, between those nuns and priests who condoned and those who disapproved of lax behaviour. It was the latter, presumably, who reported the misdeeds to the bishop. Such dissension rumbled beneath the election of the next abbess after Joan died. The bishop wrote to the prioress and convent in 1394 urging them to disregard the promptings of flesh and blood, threats, improper promises and agreements, and to elect freely an abbess of religious life and holy living. This was not the first time there had been disagreement within the community. In the periods 1216–23 and 1242–3 there were disputed elections for abbess. In 1298 the rector of Dinton was sent in as a peacemaker when the bishop learnt that the majority of the convent bore a grudge against certain nuns. And around 1317 Bishop Martival had to intervene by sending in adjudicators to settle a dispute between the abbess and some of her nuns over the repositioning of the high altar.[20]

By trawling the sources of medieval monastic history – principally the state papers and the bishops' registers – for specific references to Shaftesbury Abbey, we are left with an impression of a community made up of neither saints nor sinners, but of real, believable women, with a healthy mixture of piety and mischief. And if, by virtue of the material to hand, we have emphasized too much their failings, William of Malmesbury's description of about 1120 will help to redress the balance:

> In all their manners gentle modesty so accords with gracious austerity that no-one can surpass them. It is uncertain, indeed, whether to praise most their diligence in the service of God or the pleasantness of their converse with mankind. Thus they speak the truth who claim that the world, which has long staggered under the burden of its sins, is entirely upheld by their prayers.[21]

So far in this chapter we have spoken about the community and meant the nuns. But we have seen from our tour around the precinct in chapter 4 that many other people, men and women, lived or worked in Shaftesbury Abbey who were not nuns. They were servants, priests, tradespeople and guests. If we look back at Joan Formage's will, where we began, they are there. She remembered her maid, Edith, her chamberlain, usher, pantryman and butler; small sums went also to the kitchen valets, Cabezow and Pope, to her porter, to the pages of her chamber, and to her servant Walter. What else can we find out about them?[22]

The corrodians figure most often in the records. They were the equivalent of paying guests, who enjoyed board and lodging for life. Their payment might be the rent of a property, or employment at some task within the precinct. They might be priests who were temporary corrodians while awaiting preferment to a living within the abbess's gift. Or they might be entertained in return for some favour to the abbey, or to the king – who had the right to nominate corrodians. The terms of their tenure illuminate not only their standard of living, but also that of the nuns. The king's nominees were elderly servants or their widows. Maud Cuylly, widow of the king's armourer, was nominated in 1346, and Joan Bray, his physician's widow, in 1377. Other beneficiaries were the sealer of writs in the king's chancery, Richard Knyght, in 1329, and a yeoman of the chamber, Henry Ley, in 1451. Sometimes the benefits were spelled out. Juliana la Despensere in 1310 could expect the necessaries of life according to the requirements of her estate for herself and a damsel serving her, and a chamber to dwell in. John Goldwegge's entitlement in 1413 was a convent loaf and a pot of convent ale daily (as the nuns have), sixpence every Friday for provisions, seven shillings' clothing allowance at Christmas and Midsummer, and white salt and oatmeal at Christmas from the kitchener. Roger de Melbury in 1329 also received bread and ale daily, and a dish from the kitchen, but in return he was in charge of the copper, silver and brazen vessels in the kitchen, where he worked. A more responsible post, that of abbey gatekeeper, in 1351 seems to have deserved a more substantial

Work in the kitchen, a drawing by Frank Garbutt.

corrody – bread, ale, flesh, fish, brushwood, provender and oats, as well as the gatekeeper's perquisites.[23]

All nunneries required the presence of male priests, since only men could officiate at religious services. Chaplains were employed for this and other spiritual tasks, such as the nuns' confessor. A bond of trust developed between an abbess and her chaplain, and we have seen how Joan Formage favoured the

A priest officiating at the high altar, a drawing by Frank Garbutt.

mass priest who would pray for her soul. At Shaftesbury there were many chaplains attached to the chantries within the abbey church, as well as priests (appointed by the abbess) in the town churches and further afield. In addition several of the older and richer Wessex nunneries had prebends attached to them. There were four in the case of Shaftesbury, linked to the parishes of Iwerne Minster, Fontmell Magna, Gillingham and distant Liddington in north Wiltshire. The principle of a prebend was that the income from parish tithes would support a priest (or prebendary) to serve in the abbey church, while leaving the parish in the care of a lower paid vicar. In practice the prebends became sinecures, their holders appointing a vicar to serve in the parish and another at the abbey, linked with other duties. A complicated situation arose in 1325 when Stephen Prowet, the prebendary of Fontmell, who employed vicars to serve on his behalf in the abbey and parish, wished to exchange livings with the rector of a parish in Bath and Wells diocese. Enquiries, involving two bishops and an archdeacon, were needed before it was determined that the incoming prebendary would be suitable for the post.[24]

Just as for its spiritual needs, so for its material comforts the abbey endowed officials with an income from the lands under its control. By the twelfth century landholdings linked to duties within the abbey (known as sergeanties) included that of the baker (at Compton Abbas), the mason (at Melbury Abbas), the cook (at Cann), the butler (possibly Totterdale in Wardour), and the porter (perhaps in Bradford on Avon). These duties probably ceased,

The grave slab of Thomas Scalis, with his epitaph extolling in Latin his kindness and generosity.

from an early date, to be performed by the landholder in person, and became honorific. But male officials continued to play an important role in the abbey's life right up to the dissolution. Two laymen, Alexander Cater the sacrist, and Stephen Payne the steward, were granted the distinction of burial within the abbey. They shared this honour with a third man, a priest, whose grave slab was discovered by Wilson Claridge and is now on display in the abbey museum. He was Thomas Scalis, who died in 1532. His Latin epitaph celebrates his kindness and generosity to the poor, giving food, drink and money from his store.[25]

The epitaph of Alexander Cater, sacrist.

For the men and women of seven centuries whose lives revolved around this windswept hill Shaftesbury Abbey was a place of worship, work and confinement. But beyond the convent wall was a wider world, no less important, no less relevant to our theme.

Looking south from Park Walk across Blackmore Vale.

6 The Business of a Nunnery

LIKE SOME VICTORIAN INDUSTRIALIST surveying from his hilltop mansion the factory where his wealth was made, so the abbess of Shaftesbury could look out across the pleasant countryside – Dorset to the south, Wiltshire to the north – and feel reassured. The oxen ploughing the Compton fields, the sheep on Melbury Down, the mills and fisheries along the Stour, the windswept trees on the Donhead hillside – nearly everywhere, as far as the eye could see and further, was trickling its profits to her abbey, and enabling her nuns to continue their lives of sophisticated devotion. And from farms and cottages across Blackmore Vale her tenants could scan the distant ridge for the abbey tower and know that, whether they liked it or not, God had so ordered their world that Shaftesbury Abbey was its summit.

For the townspeople also, who regarded themselves a freer race than their feudal rustic colleagues, there must have been the recognition that ultimately they too were shackled to the abbey gates. The abbess controlled much of the town's trade, was the largest owner of town properties, and from her home farm employed labourers to cultivate a portion of the town's surrounding farmland. Furthermore, the abbey's presence brought pilgrims, strangers and officials to Shaftesbury, who in turn brought money and goods, news and excitement from the wider world. Medieval abbeys are rightly seen as spiritual and academic powerhouses, but they could only function as such because they were also the headquarters of business empires.

Shaftesbury Abbey's most lucrative estates were all acquired before the Norman conquest, either at the time of its foundation, or as subsequent gifts by kings and benefactors. We have already described the circumstances of some of these acquisitions. But it continued to amass land, rights and services through the middle ages, often as a form of dowry given by the families of girls destined to take the veil and enter the community. Written surveys exist of this portfolio at various stages in the abbey's history, and from these we can see its geographical spread and gauge the importance of each of its components.[1]

The heartland of the abbey estate was an almost continuous block of land straddling the Dorset–Wiltshire border, and extending from Iwerne Minster some 9km south of Shaftesbury beneath the Cranborne Chase escarpment, to Chicklade on the Wiltshire chalklands 12km to the north. Within this block were islands of property, such as Semley, which never belonged to the abbey; in most cases this was because they had been granted at an early date to other powerful religious bodies, such as Wilton Abbey or the bishops of Winchester.

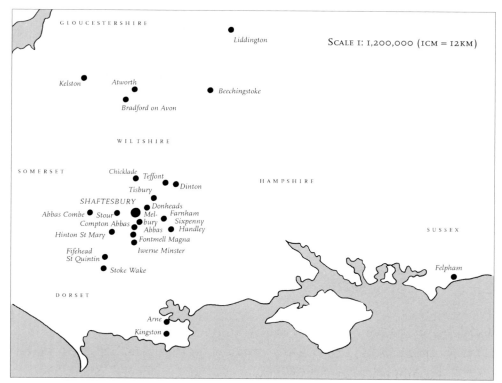

The principal estates of Shaftesbury Abbey (see also map on page 20).

But (these anomalies aside) it is striking how closely Shaftesbury Abbey's home territory corresponds with the catchment area of the modern town as a service provider – an enduring legacy of the Saxon era which is easily overlooked.

The abbey's inheritance, then as now, embraced a diverse and beautiful countryside, offering a range of agricultural and natural resources. To the south it controlled a ribbon of settlements – Melbury, Compton, Fontmell and Iwerne – whose lands extended along the eastern edge of Blackmore Vale, from the heavy Kimmeridge clay of Hardy's 'valley of the little dairies', up the hollowed wooded hillsides of greensand and on to the chalk downland sheepwalks of Cranborne Chase. Other communities, Hinton St Mary, East and West Stour, sat on the valley floor further west. The streams which water these villages flow south to feed the Dorset Stour, and the Shaftesbury ridge forms a watershed. To the north, although the geological components and sequence are the same, the headwaters of another river system have created an altogether more broken and intricate scenery, around Tisbury and the Donheads, and in places have exposed the Portland beds of fine building stone. This is the River Nadder, flowing eastwards to Salisbury, and here in its valley, the Vale of Wardour, is a rather more scattered settlement pattern of hamlets and farms.[2]

Beyond the abbey's heartland were other manors. Some, such as Sixpenny Handley on Cranborne Chase, Teffont in the Vale of Wardour, or Stoke Wake and Fifehead St Quintin on the far side of Blackmore Vale, shared the same characteristics, and lay at no great distance from Shaftesbury, 20km at most. But others were more remote, such as the north Wiltshire estate of Liddington overlooking the Thames Valley, whose pastures have now disappeared beneath Swindon housing estates; or Felpham in West Sussex, which has become part of the seaside resort of Bognor Regis. Another coastland possession was Kingston on the Isle of Purbeck near Corfe Castle. These, and other less important outliers, had probably come to the abbey for the most part through family connections of Shaftesbury nuns. But one of the largest and most lucrative acquisitions, as we saw in chapter 3, was the result of a political decision during a national emergency. This was Bradford on Avon in Wiltshire, at the southern end of the Cotswolds, and not far from Bath. Like Tisbury and Iwerne it continued an earlier monastic estate, and included a whole group of villages and hamlets surrounding a small town at an important river-crossing.

Bradford in the middle ages was destined to become not only a major source of grain for the abbey, but it also developed flourishing industries in clothmaking and stone-quarrying.[3]

Fontmell, 5km south of Shaftesbury, provides a good example of the way in which the abbey acquired and then managed and exploited, one of its properties. We know about its acquisition not from the original charter, but from a copy written in the fifteenth century into the abbey's cartulary, a kind of manuscript ledger (now in the British Library) which served as the medieval equivalent of a filing cabinet. From its wording it appears (unlike many) to be a faithful copy, and it tells us that at Amesbury on Christmas Eve 932 AD King Aethelstan, witnessed by the archbishops of Canterbury and York, granted 'to his most faithful community of nuns who serve God under the rule of practising the life of devotion in the city which is called Shaftesbury', an estate of 11½ hides in a place which the inhabitants call *Funtemel*. So that there could be no argument it was common with such grants for the boundaries of the land in question to be described in great detail, along hedgerows, across fields and over streams. Close comparison of the Saxon names in this boundary list with modern names in the area suggests that the land described was identical to the medieval and modern parish of Fontmell Magna.[4]

We next hear of Shaftesbury's Fontmell estate 150 years later in Domesday Book (1086). The taxable assessment had grown to 15 hides (a hide was computed to be the amount of land needed to support one extended household), and about one-fifth was farmed directly for the abbey by its servants. The remainder was tenanted to no fewer than 65 inhabitants and their families. They cultivated the arable land with fourteen ploughteams, had a share of meadow, pasture and woodland, and took their corn for grinding to one of the abbey's three mills on the estate.[5]

The bald statistics of Domesday Book are fleshed out some fifty years later by the earlier of two surveys of the abbey estates. Both surveys are contained in the cartulary, and can be dated to about 1130 and 1170. From them we learn the Fontmell tenants' names (good Saxon names such as Winegot, Elwin and Brichmer), the extent of their holdings, and the services they had to render to the abbey in return for their feudal tenancies. At the later date Semer, Ailnoth, William and eight other tenants were all in possession of a virgate of land (¼ of a hide) for which they paid ten pence annual rent and twenty pence for the right to take timber from the abbey's woods. They also had to reap and carry two acres during harvesting in August, mow the meadow at haymaking and cart the corn. Specialists, such as the millers, the ploughmen and the pig-keeper had slightly different obligations. Robert the smith, for example, held his half-virgate in return for making ploughshares and horseshoes for the abbey's team, as well as ploughing, sowing and reaping duties. The century since the conquest seems to have been a time of modest expansion at Fontmell. There were now 80 tenants, of whom 55 held either a virgate or half-virgate, and a fourth mill had been added to the three recorded in Domesday Book.[6]

Across the abbey's entire estate, of course, the total number of tenants was very large. Some were themselves important proprietors, and the land they held as abbey tenants was only a small part of their total possessions. Such men owed service to the abbess of various kinds. As a major landowner she had an obligation to keep fighting men (knights) in readiness for military service; landholdings were set aside to support such men, and the tenants of 'knight's fees', as these holdings were known, were required to discharge the abbess's military duty (themselves or by proxy) on her behalf. Depending on the circumstances of their tenure they might perform other services as well, and these are stipulated in the twelfth-century surveys. One had to supply a rope for the well at Shaftesbury, another had to lend his cart to carry hay to the hall, several others had to act as messengers, riding errands for the abbess.[7]

One small manor had a specialist function that was essential to preserving the nuns' food supply. This was Arne, on the edge of Poole Harbour, which formed part of the abbey's Kingston estate on Purbeck. Here, according to the later twelfth-century survey, were twenty-two households, each possessing one or more (or a share in one) *plumbum*. The word means 'lead vat', and they were salt-workers. Their thirst-making and somewhat obnoxious livelihoods were earned by washing sea-salt from the sand flats and boiling the resulting brine in their vats until all the water was driven off. A proportion (perhaps one-tenth) of their output was demanded by the abbey in addition to a money rent, and it was an obligation on other tenants, from Fontmell and Iwerne, to travel to Arne with their carts and collect it.[8]

Part of the court roll of the abbess's manor of Tisbury, 1349. The word mort' *('died') can be seen against many of the tenants' names (WSRO 2667/13/530).*

Court rolls have survived for the abbess's manor of Tisbury for certain years during the fourteenth century. Two, dated April 1348 and April 1349, provide a striking indication of the workforce on a single estate. At the head of the earlier roll a list is given of all the (probably landless) tenants due to pay a head-tax at the court. Eighty individuals are named, of whom three had died during the previous year. The equivalent list, made in April 1349, makes sombre reading. There were 78 names this year, but against 43 of them no sum was given, simply the word *mort'* ('dead'). The Black Death had engulfed Tisbury. It was a devastating tragedy for the local community, and for many like it; but epidemics (human and animal) could also create economic havoc for the abbey. In 1381, beset by pestilence among her tenants and their cattle, the abbess was facing bankruptcy, if we are to believe her appeal to the king for relief.[9]

Despite these crises the best demonstration of the tenantry working smoothly in the service of Shaftesbury Abbey as a business also comes from the later fourteenth century. An account roll has survived of the group of communities centred on Bradford on Avon, for five years between 1367 and 1392. Bradford is some 60km north of Shaftesbury, and it is likely that the abbess seldom, if ever, visited it. Her interests there were supervised by a steward based at Barton Farm, close to the town centre, and beneath him by bailiffs and reeves of the individual manors which made up this west Wiltshire group. The steward was responsible for collecting money payments to the abbey, derived from rents for specific holdings, dues from lessees of certain manorial enterprises (such as

Bradford on Avon, the so-called tithe barn attached to the abbey's Barton Farm.

fisheries, dovecotes and bakeries), and cash paid in lieu of labour services which had been commuted. He also oversaw the abbey's employees on the demesne (or 'home') farm, including drovers, carters, shepherds, a maltster, a pig-keeper and others. At haymaking and harvest the abbey tenants were called on to supplement the regular staff. One portion of the corn grown on the home farm was used locally, to barter for other goods and services, while the remainder was sent to Shaftesbury, either as grain or as malt for brewing.[10]

Livestock farming was an important component of the abbey's Bradford demesne. In 1367 there were 129 cattle including 51 oxen used as draught animals. There were also nearly 1,000 sheep, kept foremost for their wool, and the flock seems to have been reared in conjunction with another Bradford manor, Liddington near Swindon, which had a generous acreage of rough downland pasture. Bradford could provide the abbey with other commodities, too. Like Kingston on Purbeck and Tisbury in Wardour Vale it was an important source of building stone; it was involved in the woollen trade as well, and the abbey derived rent from its fulling mills. Timber, eels, salted bacon and palm branches (for use on Palm Sunday) were all taken by cart or packhorse to Shaftesbury, along with consignments of grain, malt and stone. In 1367, according to the account, there appear to have been 622 such journeys made through the miry claylands of Selwood Forest and over the exposed chalk downland of south-west Wiltshire.

The estates of an abbey, and the revenues accruing from them, were known as temporalities. But Shaftesbury, like any other religious foundation, could also derive 'spiritual' income from various sources, such as the parish churches it controlled, and from legacies given in return for prayers (known as 'obits') made in intercession for the dead. Gillingham, Shaftesbury's north Dorset neighbour, is a good example of such a spirituality. William the Conqueror gave the abbey the church on his royal manor of Gillingham as compensation for taking some of the abbey's land on Purbeck to build Corfe Castle. The abbey, as we saw in chapter 5, used this gift to nominate and support a priest (known as a prebendary) who both served Gillingham parishioners and acted as a chaplain to the abbey community. In about 1318 the then prebendary appointed a vicar (the word means deputy) to undertake his duties at Gillingham, at a stipend much lower than the total revenue from the church.[11] Other churches belonged to the abbey (and some were made prebends in the same way as Gillingham), either because they were on the community's own estates, such as Bradford or Tisbury, or because they had been given as a form of dowry by fathers and other relatives of prospective nuns. Thus around 1100 a Norman landowner in Devon, Odo fitz Gamelin, gave the abbey his church at Great Torrington on behalf of two daughters; another Norman magnate, Ernulf de Hesding, gave Keevil church in Wiltshire on behalf of a relative. Much later, in about 1395, the abbey was able to benefit from his generosity in another way. They sold all their rights to Keevil church for £133 in order to bolster the endowment of a recently founded monastic house at nearby Edington.[12]

We have seen in chapter 5 that some religious activities in the medieval church, such as administering the sacrament, could only be performed by men. It was therefore essential that the nunnery retained a group of priests and chaplains, and the endowment of prebends such as Gillingham was an efficient way of doing this. Others were supplied by the chantry system, which became not only a particularly significant part of religious life in the later middle ages (as we have discussed), but also served to augment the abbey's landholdings. In a typical case Sibyl Cokyn and Agnes de Hacche, with their husbands, set up a fund in 1334 to pay for a priest to pray for their souls, and those of their ancestors and heirs, at the altar of St Thomas in the abbey church. The income was derived from the rent of three houses in Shaftesbury, together with arable and meadow land. There were many such chantry priests celebrating obits daily, some on behalf of former abbesses, others for families from Shaftesbury and elsewhere. No fewer than 22 names between 1342 and 1465 have been recorded for one such endowment; prayers continued to be

Chicksgrove manor house, on the abbess's Tisbury estate.

said at several chantry chapels and altars right up until the day the abbey was dissolved.[13]

It is a paradox that, although the abbey complex at Shaftesbury was comprehensively flattened within a few years of the nuns' departure, some of the most impressive buildings that enabled them to function as a rich and successful community have survived. If we look beyond the precinct we shall find survivors, fragmentary or complete, scattered across the Dorset and Wiltshire estates. There are the remains of abbey tenants' houses, Higher Farm at Margaret Marsh, and the manor house at Hinton St Mary (both in Blackmore Vale), as well as Leigh Court at Donhead St Andrew, and Gaston and Chicksgrove Manors at Tisbury. There are large medieval barns at Atworth (on the Bradford estate), Kelston (near Bath) and Hinton St Mary; a church house (the equivalent of a parish hall) in Bradford, and possibly another at Donhead St

The gatehouse of Place Farm, Tisbury.

Mary (now Pilgrim's Cottage); and of course much surviving medieval architecture and fittings in the churches which belonged to the abbey. The farmhouse which controlled the demesne agriculture on the Donhead estate is now called Berry Court Farm, and it still straddles the boundary between the two parishes into which the estate was divided.

But far and away the most impressive survivals are the two complexes of farming and administrative buildings, known as granges, which controlled the abbey's principal outlying estates – Place Farm at Tisbury, and Barton Farm at Bradford. Much of medieval Place Farm survives, and anyone approaching

The thatched barn at Place Farm, Tisbury.

Tisbury from the east is greeted by the magnificent sight of its thatched barn, a leviathan some 61 metres long. The fourteenth-century farmhouse, used by the abbess herself as a country residence, is hidden from the road by a contemporary gatehouse. This led into a farmyard surrounded by stables (which were demolished in the nineteenth century) and by a second gatehouse beyond. The outer gate is large enough to give access to laden medieval wagons on their way to and from the barn, but the inner gatehouse is for pedestrians only. At the dissolution the abbess's house had eight rooms, a chapel and various outbuildings surrounded by a wall. Nearby were fishponds and a mill.[15]

The barn at Place Farm, like its smaller counterpart (a mere 52 metres long) at Barton Farm, Bradford, is often wrongly described as a tithe barn. In fact both would have been used to accumulate the produce of the demesne farm as well as tithes and other payments in kind. They were the equivalent of

Late-medieval bridge across the River Avon at Bradford, giving access to the Barton Farm complex of Shaftesbury Abbey buildings.

modern storage depots. Surviving buildings of the abbey's grange at Bradford include, beside the famous barn, a farmhouse (extended in the eighteenth century) and a granary, together occupying three sides of a courtyard. The presence of another medieval barn, on the fourth side, was revealed by excavation after a later building had been damaged by fire. This complex, and the adjacent bridge across the River Avon, are all believed to date from the early fourteenth century, and are now publicly accessible as the centrepiece of a country park.[16]

In our hunt for tangible remains of the abbey's impact on its medieval surroundings we are apt to overlook survivals of a different kind. Compton Abbas and Melbury Abbas, as well as Abbas Combe in Somerset, owe half their names to the fact that the abbess of Shaftesbury owned them. Hinton takes its affix (St Mary) not from the dedication of its own church, but from that of the abbey; Margaret Marsh may be named after one of the fourteenth-century abbesses; and Minchington, near Handley, means 'farm of the nuns'.[17]

Monastic control implanted on the communities it owned not only the names we still use today, but to a large extent also the shape of villages, the pattern of their lanes and the arrangement of their fields. Much remains to be discovered about the revolution which seems to have occurred between the tenth and twelfth centuries, and which involved the creation of nucleated settlements and the system of large open fields farmed in common. But it was happening everywhere across southern England at precisely the period when Shaftesbury Abbey was acquiring and consolidating its landholdings. Some ecclesiastical landlords, such as Glastonbury Abbey and the bishops of Winchester, have left evidence for village planning, along the Polden Hills in Somerset, for instance, and in Wiltshire's Ebble valley. Shaftesbury Abbey was perhaps more conservative in this respect, allowing villages such as Melbury and Iwerne to develop without apparent plan, and content to retain in places (Tisbury and the Donheads for instance) an older pattern of scattered settlement.[18]

The abbey's most profound impact was on Shaftesbury itself. We have seen in earlier chapters how the site and layout of the abbey and town are interrelated. And we shall shortly reflect on the consequences for the town of the abbey's disappearance. But it is important to recognize that Shaftesbury too was a vital part of the abbey's business empire. Not only was the busy urban sector, with its market and tradesmen and service providers, that empire's commercial lung; but the town's immediate surroundings, north to Wincombe just beyond the county boundary, east to Mampitts and south to Cann, made up the home farm, supplying the nuns with much of the food and supplies for their domestic needs.

As at Bradford (and elsewhere, for example at Marlborough) the home farm was known as Barton Farm. It was regarded in the middle ages as a separate manor, and its headquarters or grange included a thatched dwelling house for the bailiff, a barn some 50 metres long, a large cattle byre and a penning for sheep, as well as gardens and paddocks. Remains of some of the outbuildings, but not of the manor house itself, were discovered by archaeologists in 1951 in the area of the cattle market, close to Barton Hill House and the street called Barton Hill. The Barton farmland included meadow, pasture, arable and woodland, together with a large open heath. Much of it has been built over with twentieth-century housing and an industrial estate, but some of the names in current use – Crookhays, Longmead, Littledown –

Park Wall, Gold Hill, Shaftesbury.

would have been as familiar to the abbey bailiff as they are to present-day Shastonians.[19]

One rather more specialist farming activity, the raising and killing of deer and other game for the abbess's aristocratic table, has also left its mark on the modern landscape. The abbey maintained two parks in the vicinity of the town. Wincombe, to the north and on the Wiltshire side of the county boundary adjoining Gillingham Forest, was a 60 acre deer park with hare warren administered as part of Barton Farm. Much smaller (only a few acres, and probably intended for exercise and privacy more than for venison) was the park which lay right on the abbey's doorstep, falling away below Park Walk and giving Gold Hill the gentle sloping curve for which it is world famous. Here the massive retaining wall, some 600 years old and the subject of countless photographs, is for those who appreciate it the most substantial and impressive reminder in Shaftesbury itself of the abbey's former domination.[20]

7 Disintegration

I N 1496, WHEN THE FUTURE KING HENRY VIII was a five-year-old prince, the nuns of Shaftesbury elected from their number a new abbess. Margery (or Margaret) Twinhoe was chosen to preside over a community of 36 nuns, the lowest recorded total in the abbey's medieval history. At least nine of them must have been relatively old, since they had been present at the previous election in 1460, 36 years earlier. The new abbess came of a gentry family from near Frome in Somerset, but with local connections. Her father had served as MP for Shaftesbury and other family members were active in the area. She had a clergyman brother, Christopher, who acted as her steward, and to whom she bestowed several livings in her gift; he went on to become Archdeacon of Berkshire. Margery and Christopher discovered that the abbey's archives were in a mess, 'not arranged by manors . . . but very confusedly in divers chests and boxes', and they helped the sacristan to compile a new register. By the end of her short reign (she died in 1504 or 1505) there were 50 nuns, and (as we have seen) she had been honoured to entertain, in 1501, the future queen Catherine of Aragon, on her journey from Plymouth to London to marry Henry's older brother, Prince Arthur.[1]

These miscellaneous facts about an otherwise obscure abbess help to illustrate what was happening to the English nunneries as the middle ages drew to a close. Relatively few aristocratic girls now took the veil of their own volition or at their family's behest. No more the favoured resort of noble ladies, therefore, Shaftesbury was in the charge of a local squire's daughter, who used her position to further relatives' careers. The number of nuns had dropped from over 100 in the thirteenth century, and the paperwork was neglected probably because the abbey no longer farmed most of its estate directly, but leased the manors out for a money rent. The leasing of demesnes, which occurred very widely during the fifteenth century, seems to have been adopted quite late by Shaftesbury Abbey. The abbess's manor of Tisbury was farmed directly until about 1470, and the sheep flocks of several home farms continued to be managed by the abbey right up to the end. The switch to leasing, when and where it came, brought benefits both to the landowner – simplified administration and a comparatively certain income – and to the lessee, who was given freedom to innovate, and thereby potentially to rise from small farmer to landed gentry. But it also sidelined the abbess, so far as her tenants' loyalties were concerned, and fragmented her estate. Spiritually, however earnest and pious the nuns of Shaftesbury remained, theological thinking within the established church and at its frontiers was moving away from the monastic ideal and towards the protestant overthrow. For the Tudor government abbeys such as Shaftesbury were most useful for the hospitality they were bound to provide.[2]

Within the world of late-medieval monasticism nunneries played a relatively small part. In 1535 there were only about 1,900 nuns in England (compared with nearly 9,000 monks, friars and canons), and most of the 137 nunneries were very small and quite poor. In fact only 21 scored above the threshold of £200 annual income which came to differentiate the larger from the smaller monasteries. But six of these lay in the Wessex heartland of Wiltshire, Dorset and Hampshire, and by far the largest was Shaftesbury. With 57 nuns in 1535 and an income of £1,166, it compared with Wilton (33 and £601), Amesbury (34 and £525), and Romsey, Wherwell and Tarrant, with between 20 and 26 nuns apiece. No English nunnery had more nuns than Shaftesbury and only one, Syon in Middlesex, was wealthier. By comparison, there were 17 male monasteries with incomes over £1,000. Nunneries in general, therefore, had become places of little significance (and many were struggling to continue), but Shaftesbury was one of the few exceptions.[3]

In 1529 Elizabeth Zouche became the last abbess of Shaftesbury (although such a description would have astonished her at the time). In her cloister she would doubtless have pondered the future of English monasticism, fretted over the difficulties facing nunneries large and small, and speculated on the ominous machinations at court. But any such worries were rapidly engulfed by a chain of international events. Henry, frustrated at the pope's refusal to declare his marriage to Catherine unlawful, began through legislation to curtail Rome's control over the English church. In 1533 the archbishop of Canterbury, no longer answerable to the pope, annulled Henry's marriage, and in 1534 by the Act of Supremacy the king became head of the (still Catholic) church of England. Bishops, clergy, heads of religious houses (including Elizabeth), monks and nuns had little choice but to acknowledge Henry's authority, and most did so without demur. The wealth of the English church, its lands, buildings, revenues and spiritualities, all thereby came within the king's control, who was thus free to reorganize its financial and administrative structures as he saw fit.

The religious houses found themselves in a difficult position, since they stood largely outside the hierarchy of bishops and parishes, and had until then been answerable directly to the pope. They were widely seen at court, and probably in the country as a whole, as anachronistic and pointless, with no relevant part to play within a revitalized English church. And although individual houses might feel poor (nunneries especially) as they struggled to maintain buildings and fulfil spiritual obligations, the landholding and revenues of monasteries overall made this sector of the church very rich indeed.

In 1535 the government took an inventory of ecclesiastical wealth, including the monasteries, and the following year began the process of dissolving the smaller houses (below the £200 annual income threshold). Although the pretext for this action was the supposedly lax conduct of such communities, the terms offered to the monks and nuns affected were not particularly harsh. They could move to larger monasteries, be pensioned off, or be relieved of their vows and, in the case of men, become parish priests. Most women decided to transfer, and Shaftesbury received the prioress and two nuns from a small Benedictine house at Cannington, near Bridgwater in Somerset.[4]

At this stage there seems to have been no intention to abolish the larger monasteries as well, although the readiness of most smaller houses to capitulate may have suggested it. But after organized resistance to the suppression of small monasteries in Lincolnshire and northern England was crushed in 1536–7, prudent abbots and abbesses began to contemplate the unthinkable and prepare for their own abolition. Some volunteered, most accepted with grudging resignation, a very few resisted and were hanged. By 1540 there were no monasteries functioning in England.

The king's motive in dissolving the monasteries was undoubtedly financial. Given an idealistic spin the intention might be described as unlocking the wealth vested in the obsolete (and sometimes corrupt) monasteries and diverting it to more efficient church purposes – a scheme which enjoyed a measure of popular support among the laity. Shaftesbury stood briefly to benefit from such idealism, as it included the creation of a number of suffragan bishoprics in English towns. In 1538 John Bradley, former abbot of Milton, was consecrated the first and only bishop of Shaftesbury. But good intentions were rapidly overtaken by the government's financial crisis, and during the 1540s many of the newly acquired monastic lands were sold to the *nouveaux riches* merchants and officials of Henry's England, to pay for his foreign ambitions and belligerence.[5]

It is against this background that Shaftesbury, like everywhere else, lost its abbey. Having assented to Henry's supremacy over the church in 1534, the nuns were visited by two commissions of enquiry the following year. The earlier examined the abbey's books and compiled a valuation of its wealth. The later was concerned with the morality and conduct of the nuns, but was quite unable to rake out any scandal. One potential source of embarrassment, to the government not the abbey, was anticipated and discreetly avoided. A young nun, Dorothy Clusey, who under the terms of Henry's compact with the monasteries would have been free to leave, was revealed to be the illegitimate daughter of Cardinal Wolsey. The abbess, it was suggested, should be asked to encourage her to remain incognito at Shaftesbury, which she was apparently quite content to do.[6]

The abbess, Elizabeth Zouche, appears at this stage to have adopted a compliant attitude towards the commissioners. Like Margery Twinhoe she was of local gentry stock, and her family in 1536 negotiated with the king's secretary and vicar-general, Thomas Cromwell, to acquire an ailing nearby priory, Stavordale near Bruton, when its last two canons transferred to Taunton. Perhaps in return for this favour she acceded to Cromwell's request that he be

permitted to present the next rector to Tarrant Hinton, a right that the abbey had
hitherto enjoyed. She was also on familiar terms with one of Cromwell's Dorset
commissioners, Thomas Arundell, who by 1535 was on her payroll as receiver of
rents.

But by then, as the greater abbeys began to succumb, Arundell and his
fellow-commissioner John Tregonwell were encouraging Elizabeth to surrender
the abbey. The more sympathetic Arundell seems to have felt pressurising by
Tregonwell to be counter-productive when he visited the abbey late in 1538, as
the abbess appeared to stiffen her resolve. She tried to buy them off, and
proposed the sum of £400 to allow herself and her nuns to remain in their
abbey, 'by some other name and apparel'. She held out until 1539, but by then its
closure was inevitable. On Passion Sunday, 23 March, having negotiated the
terms of the pensions to be assigned to her nuns and herself, she signed the
document of surrender presented to her by John Tregonwell, and monastic life
in Shaftesbury came to an end. Hers was the last (as well as the largest) nunnery

The eviction of the nuns, a drawing by Frank Garbutt.

to be dissolved; and since it was also the first to be founded, it could claim the longest continuous existence, some 650 years, of any English religious house for women.[7]

The quire silent after so long, the cloister deserted, the great door locked. It was one of those awesome days in history which, as everyone caught up in it must have known, meant that their world had changed. A full stop. We may speculate that there were four burning questions on the lips of Shastonians that Sunday morning: What would happen to the nuns, to the abbey buildings, to its vast estates, and to the town of Shaftesbury itself?

This last question, the effect on Shaftesbury as an urban community, can wait until chapter 8. The others must be tackled now. The least affected by the closure would certainly have been the abbey's estates. The core of the abbess's holdings, in north Dorset and south-west Wiltshire, which by her surrender she forfeited to the Crown, were acquired in two tranches by Sir Thomas Arundell, one of the commissioners who had closed the abbey down. In June 1540 he purchased Tisbury with its dependent manors and Dinton, and in September 1544 the Donheads, Melbury and Compton Abbas. The far-flung possessions, such as Bradford, went to other purchasers, and their link with Shaftesbury was severed.[8]

Sir Thomas Arundell was the younger son of Sir John Arundell of Lanherne, a branch of a gentry family which had ramified across Cornwall since its arrival with the Norman conquest. None of Sir Thomas's forbears had direct links with the Shaftesbury area, although Wardour Castle, in Tisbury parish, had been built and had descended through families to which he was related. He acquired the castle and its park from a kinsman, Fulke Greville, in 1547 – the last of his major purchases – and it became the seat of the Arundells for centuries thereafter. Born in about 1500, he had risen to prominence at court through his connection with Cardinal Wolsey, first as pupil and later as friend. Shortly after Wolsey's downfall and Henry's marriage to Anne Boleyn, Sir Thomas took Anne's cousin, Margaret Howard, as his wife. Margaret was also Catherine Howard's sister, so in due course (albeit briefly) he found himself the king's brother-in-law.[9]

Although Sir Thomas was not native to the Shaftesbury area his connection with it went back at least to 1529, when he acquired land at

Thornton near Marnhull (south-west of the town), and in the vicinity of Pulham, between Sturminster and Dorchester. Then in 1535 he purchased from an uncle two manors close to the abbey's heartland, at Tollard Royal and Farnham on Cranborne Chase. In the same year, as we have seen, he served as the receiver of rents for the abbess, and in 1538 he became the lessee of various abbey estates, including Tisbury, Donhead, Handley, and the manor and mill of Barton around

Lease to Sir Thomas Arundell of Shaftesbury Abbey estates, 1538 (WSRO 2667/3/3).

Shaftesbury itself. Whether, and if so for how long, he had been manoeuvring himself into the position of successor to the abbess's landholdings it is impossible to say. The transition from steward to owner, servant to master, was quite widespread in the west country, and many families, in the words of one historian, 'who were to be the chief beneficiaries of the dissolution were already firmly installed in the administrative affairs of the monasteries for many years before the collapse came'. From the tenants' point of view what is important is that no great change occurred; the effect on many of the Shaftesbury manors would have been similar to what now would be called a management buy-out, the profits of the business redirected, but the workforce (and the work) remaining the same.[10]

For the nuns, on the other hand, it must have been a calamitous weekend. Elizabeth Bryther had been a Shaftesbury nun for at least 56 years, since 1483 or earlier. Four other nuns, including the sub-prioress Elizabeth Monmouth, could remember taking part in electing Margery Twinhoe as their abbess as long ago as 1496, 43 years before. Three nuns were described as sick and lame. They all had their pensions, it is true, and would not starve. The rate of pensions awarded to Shaftesbury nuns, in fact, was more than twice the average for nunneries. Many of the 57 women, young and old, blinking perhaps at an alien world that Sunday morning, bore the surnames of local gentry families who, one imagines, would come to their rescue. But for nuns, unlike their male counterparts, there could be no prospect of a new career as parish priests. Marriage may have been the preferred option for some, although until 1549 a nun's vow of chastity could not be revoked, and so marriage was technically a crime – a form of incest punishable by death.[11]

The abbess's plea, it will be recalled, when dissolution was threatened, had been that they be allowed to remain 'by some other name and apparel'. She seems to have contemplated that they might continue to live as a sisterhood, although no longer as nuns. Such a desire is hardly surprising – close friendships nurtured over a lifetime of communal living were less easily destroyed than buildings. There is an increasing body of evidence to suggest that groups of nuns did live in this way after their houses were suppressed. At Shaftesbury it may be significant that the abbess in 1553 gave fifty of the former nuns a present of the value of a goose. She certainly had not lost contact with them. And when the survey of the nunnery site was conducted in 1548 two of the former nuns were found to be living in adjacent tenements near the cemetery – perhaps the remnants of a formerly larger community.[12]

The fate of the abbey buildings was a harsh one. Urban monasteries at the dissolution were particularly vulnerable to destruction. Most old-established towns already had superfluous parish churches, and did not need another. Cheek by jowl with a noisy market place the claustral buildings were unsuitable for conversion to a gentleman's mansion. Prosperous trading or industrial towns could easily find a new use for a prime site. And there was a ready market for high quality building materials. The crown also had political motives for destroying monastic fabric – by stripping off the lead and dressed stonework, and so putting their buildings beyond use, there was little danger that the dissolution would ever be reversed; and there was also the prospect of a quick and large injection of cash into government funds.

At Shaftesbury all these considerations militated against the abbey church and the conventual buildings' survival. In addition Sir Thomas

Lord Arundell's house, as depicted on the 1615 map of Shaftesbury.

Arundell, the abbey's purchaser, was himself an enthusiastic despoiler – he had removed most of Hinton Charterhouse near Bath between March and June 1539, even though the Crown had sold it to someone else! Not yet the owner of Wardour Castle (which he acquired in 1547) his intention at Shaftesbury seems to have been to demolish the abbey and build a new town house on a nearby site, using salvaged building materials. The 'fair turreted house' which he built opposite the abbey precinct at the corner of Bimport and Tout Hill, was depicted on a map of 1615 and described about then as 'the greatest ornament of the town'. It survived, latterly as a public house, the Rose and Crown, until the nineteenth century.[13]

We do not know precisely when the work of destruction began. The traveller John Leland, whose last visit to Shaftesbury probably took place in 1545, refers to the abbey and the chapter house in the past tense, but that is hardly conclusive. More graphic is a thumbnail sketch of the precinct from the south which accompanied the survey made in 1548. Of the abbey church only one of the two western towers and part of an arcade of Norman arches are shown, the latter apparently with weed growing from its shattered wall. In the foreground are toppled columns and rubble. Although the sketch may be a little later than the survey its message is clear.[14]

In 1548 and 1574, as we have seen in chapter 4, detailed surveys of the abbey precinct and what remained of its buildings were carried out in order to divide it into three equal portions. As a result of Frank Hopton's meticulous detection and deduction most buildings which then survived can be located.

The church, it seems, had gone apart from a chapel in the south transept. The chapter house perhaps remained, along with the kitchen, as well as various rooms and chambers connected with the refectory. These all lay south of the church towards the escarpment, in an area now crossed by Park Walk. They were the last relics of monastic life. And although many peripheral abbey buildings of practical and commercial value were to continue in use, by 1574 another survey referred to 'the whole site of the former monastery of Shaftesbury where the buildings have already been laid low to the ground'.[15]

Sketch of the ruined abbey church (with Holy Trinity behind) from the Pembroke estate survey made in 1548.

To the three casualties described here – estates, nuns, buildings – may be added a fourth. The distinction of being the king's brother-in-law brought power and wealth, but (in the case of Henry VIII) it lacked permanence. Sir Thomas Arundell adhered to his Catholic faith as the Court, under Henry's son, Edward VI, became Protestant. He was perceived to have supported rebellious Catholic elements and as a result was sent to the Tower of London, and executed in 1552. Paradoxically, the destroyer of Shaftesbury Abbey was the only person associated with this bastion of the old religion who may have died for his Catholic convictions. At his death Shaftesbury and his other possessions were forfeited, and passed in 1553 to another leading courtier, William Herbert, earl of Pembroke. The Arundell family recovered most of their estates during the brief Catholic swansong under Mary (1553–8), but the abbey precinct remained with the Pembrokes. Its subsequent history can be left for chapter 9, where the story of the abbey's rediscovery is told.

8 The City of a Dream

I HAVE ORDERED A BEER from the café beneath the town hall and am sitting at a table in the August sunshine looking down Gold Hill. The wall behind me, part of the town hall cellar, was built in 1826, and is an intrusion of scale on the Shaftesbury townscape. In 1539, as in 1339 and 1739, this was part of an open market place – in fact, had I been sitting here then I should probably have been in the stocks, which were placed in front of Gold Hill Cross more or less on this spot. Thomas Hardy described Shaftesbury as the city of a dream,

Crofs on Gold Hill, near the West end of S. Peter's Church.

Gold Hill Cross, with stocks, an engraving from the history of Dorset by John Hutchins.

and felt that (I paraphrase) even the stimulating atmosphere and limitless landscape seen from its heights can scarcely dispel a pensive melancholy over what has been lost.

> To this fair creation of the great Middle-Age the Dissolution was, as historians tell us, the death-knell. With the destruction of the enormous abbey the whole place collapsed in a general ruin . . .

I wonder?[1]

Hardy wrote *Jude the Obscure*, his last novel, between 1890 and 1894, and it was published in November 1895. At 'Shaston' the book's turning-point is memorably played out, and millions of readers must have absorbed his description of this town of faded glory, doomed by its abbey's fall. The inspiration for Hardy's portrayal is easily found. A local clergyman and antiquary, C H Mayo, had read a paper about Shaftesbury in July 1893 to a meeting of the Dorset Field Club (to which Hardy belonged), and in 1894 it was published in the Club's *Proceedings*. Mayo wrote of, 'the fatal hour of dissolution', and, 'from that day Shaftesbury went down'. 'Well may the Shastonians of to-day', he concluded, 'make the old Park wall their "wailing place" for glories never destined to return.' My beer has arrived, and I am musing, as I look down that same old Park wall, whether Hardy and Mayo were right. What effect *did* the dissolution have on the town of Shaftesbury, and what testimony of that event can I find in the streets and buildings around me today? [2]

We must begin with the late-medieval town. The great period of urbanisation across southern England had come to an end by about 1300, and a few decades later, in 1334, it is possible through taxation records to compare the wealth of towns. Shaftesbury easily topped the Dorset list, almost as wealthy as the next two contenders (Weymouth and Bridport) combined. Only four towns in south-west England (excluding Bristol) were assessed more highly, with Salisbury at the head of the list (almost quadrupling Shaftesbury), and Exeter second. Shaftesbury was exceeded also by Plymouth and Bridgwater, and on a par with Bodmin and Wells. Similar comparisons are possible in 1377 and 1524, and these show Shaftesbury losing its pre-eminent position. At the former date the town seems to have been overtaken by its neighbour, Mere (although its total would have included Mere's large rural parish). By the latter date two Dorset towns exceeded Shaftesbury in their taxpaying assessment of wealth – Poole and Dorchester – although Shaftesbury may still have had a greater population than Dorchester, which stood at around 1,000.[3]

Gold Hill, flanked by the Park Wall.

There could be several reasons for this relative decline. The towns which were overtaking Shaftesbury in the fifteenth century were successful trading and fishing ports, or were involved in the growing cloth manufacturing industry. Such places prospered at the expense of the older traditional market centres. There is, to be sure, a little evidence of clothmaking in late-medieval Shaftesbury. John Botyler, a Shaftesbury weaver, was of sufficient standing in the community (despite a conviction in 1460 for playing dice illegally) to be elected bailiff in 1471. He had a house in Mill Lane (now Haimes Lane) which in 1494 he conveyed to trustees, probably to set up a chantry after his death. John Cockes, a tucker (i.e. fuller) of Melbury, featured in several property transactions during the 1440s, and a fulling mill at Cann was operating before 1459 and as late as 1550. Up to 1490 John Shoil, described as a mercer (i.e. cloth merchant), was part-owner of this mill. He served as constable in 1460, mayor of Shaftesbury in 1470, and one of the town's MPs in 1472. In 1444 another Shaftesbury merchant, Thomas

Predi, imported through Southampton six balets (perhaps half a ton or more) of woad, used in dyeing cloth blue.[4]

But the woad's destination was not Shaftesbury; it was carted to Downton on the River Avon south of Salisbury. And this perhaps highlights our town's difficulty. The late-medieval cloth industry sprang up in places with abundant and reliable water supplies, for washing and dyeing wool, and for turning the all-important fulling mills, which felted and cleansed the cloth. Water was not a commodity Shaftesbury was blessed with. Worse, because it affected the town's status as a marketing centre, was the fact that towns thriving on cloth, notably Salisbury, but to a lesser extent Wilton, Warminster, Sherborne and Mere, also held markets (and very vigorous markets, too, at Salisbury and Warminster) which were close enough to deflect trade from parts of Shaftesbury's catchment area.

There may have been other factors contributing to Shaftesbury's fall from pre-eminence among Dorset towns at this time. We have noted a decline in numbers at the abbey, from a peak of over 120 nuns to 50 by 1500; and also the shift to leasing, rather than farming directly, the abbey estates. Both trends must have reduced the opportunities for townspeople to be employed by the abbey or sell it their services. The nature of pilgrimage, too, although popular right up to the dissolution, was changing. The cults of Mary and Corpus Christi grew in popularity, and deflected attention away from the old-established shrines, such as Shaftesbury, where saints' relics had been venerated for centuries. At the same time theological movements within the medieval church, notably Lollardy (and ultimately Protestantism) began to attack the underlying superstitions upon which pilgrimage was based.[5]

We must set against this rather pessimistic (Hardyesque, perhaps) view of late-medieval Shaftesbury some of the evidence to be derived from its own borough records, and elsewhere. Compared with many other towns the survival of local documents from this period is poor, but we can glimpse tradesmen at work (especially when they broke the rules), the development of a local bureaucracy, and the normal conflicts and allegiances of urban society. We can also detect the skeleton of streets, open spaces and suburbs which underlies the present-day town.

Although it had not achieved autonomy from its manorial owners, the crown and the abbess, Shaftesbury in the fourteenth century took upon itself the trappings of self-government, with a mayor, bailiff, coroners and constables. The jury of the manorial court, which was nominally presided over by the king's steward, became in practice the equivalent of a corporation, which elected its officers, punished misdemeanours and decided policy. It appears to have controlled its own finances, possessed lands from which it derived rents, and to have built itself a guildhall (with blind-house or lock-up beneath) at the top end of the abbess's wall along Gold Hill. To administer its property it appointed wardens. Whatever its legal status, in practice it probably functioned as Shaftesbury's local government, merchant guild (hence the 'guildhall') and religious fellowship rolled into one, with the same leading townspeople involved in each of its aspects.[6]

So, for example, we find John Poticary in 1444 listed as one of the trustees of a property in Gold Hill known as 'Kilpecks-place'. It adjoined St Peter's Church, and the present Sun and Moon Cottage is on its site. It had been in the Kilpeck family since 1398, and was presumably (from its name) the family home. Two generations later John Kilpeck entrusted it in his will to Poticary and others to

Sun and Moon Cottage, at the top of Gold Hill, with St Peter's church tower behind.

endow an obit (an arrangement whereby a priest was paid to pray regularly for his soul) in St Peter's after his wife's death. John Kilpeck was described as a Bristol goldsmith, and one of the executors of his will was another goldsmith. Poticary seems to have been a Shaftesbury merchant (his alternative name was Mercer). He owned the fulling mill referred to earlier, and he may have had premises in Gold Hill – in 1447 he was reported to the court for leaving two pieces of wood lying there to the annoyance of John Bishopston. He was also a dealer in foreign goods through Southampton. In 1449 he imported a barrel of olive oil, a butt (over 500 litres) of sweet

Greek wine and about 25 kilos of almonds. He, like Kilpeck, wanted prayers said for his soul, and so in 1459 entrusted to a group of fellow townsmen the income from the fulling mill to endow his obit.[7]

Examples of men such as Poticary can be multiplied from the records. John Wynnyngham, for instance, was described as a clerk, and was the warden of the almshouse, the hospital of St John the Baptist. He occupied land in Coppice Lane which belonged to the hospital, and purchased a neighbour's plot in 1450. Four years earlier his neighbourliness had been called into question when he was indicted for leaving rubbish next to St John's. He died in 1470, whereafter another John Wynnyngham (perhaps his son) appears in the records in the same area of Shaftesbury. He seems to have had a similarly ambivalent attitude to the rule of law. In 1487 he was elected one of the two constables, but the following year, while still in post, people complained that he was contaminating East Street (i.e. Salisbury Street) with dung and the chaff winnowed from his grain.[8]

These glimpses of town life, set against a gradual decline – comparatively speaking – in Shaftesbury's fortunes, prepare us for the shock of the dissolution. But far from the 'general ruin' imagined by Hardy, life seems to have gone on as usual, and in some ways to have improved. Dorset's first historian, Thomas Gerard, described the town some eighty years later, in the 1620s; his observations are particularly astute, and can provide a framework for understanding what happened to Shaftesbury after 1539. He wrote:

> ... and when that fatall thunder clappe overthrewe the goodlie monasterie and church, it soe shaked the other churches, that onlie foure of them are standing at this daye. Neverthelesse the towne which still remaines is a faire thorough faire, much frequented by travellers to and from London; governed by a maior, well inhabited, and accommodated with a plentifull markett on Saturdayes.

We should consider these five points made by Gerard: religious change, a flourishing passing trade, self-government, an orderly population and a successful market; and add a sixth, the general rebuilding of the town.[9]

The four churches mentioned by Gerard must be St Peter's (at the top of Gold Hill), Holy Trinity (in Bimport), St Rumbold's (Salisbury Street), and St James's, below the escarpment. All still stand, though three were rebuilt by the Victorians and only two, St Peter's and St James's, are still used for worship.

They are the survivors of twelve which existed around 1300 (Gerard knew of ten), but six had gone out of use long before the reformation, and only two, St Martin's in Angel Square and St Laurence's in Bell Street, were casualties of the religious changes in the sixteenth century. Like St Peter's, both were controlled by the abbey, who presented rectors to their livings, and after the reformation their parishes were subsumed within expanded parishes of St Peter's and Holy Trinity. During the sixteenth century St Peter's church was enlarged, with the building of a new south aisle, and reroofed.[10]

Many Saxon towns found themselves over-provided with churches as the middle ages wore on. Had Shaftesbury not possessed so many there might have been a chance that the abbey church would have survived. But two for the town and two for the suburbs proved quite sufficient. The real impact of the religious upheaval was not where, but how, people worshipped, and what ancillary activities, such as schooling, pageantry and poor relief, were swept away along with the old beliefs.

St Peter's church began to adopt the protestant simplicity which it retains today. Its new south aisle contrived to make it light and almost square,

St Peter's, the only medieval church to survive in Shaftesbury. To its right is the Town Hall of 1826-7, which stands at the top of Gold Hill.

whitewashed walls replaced gaudy murals, panelling hid the scars where images were removed, pulpit and communion table supplanted the high altar. For some the reforms were inadequate; as in other Wessex towns, Puritan elements in Shaftesbury challenged the sitting incumbent, and in 1617 used a legal technicality to introduce a rival minister of radical leanings. This battle continued for some years. But one relic of medieval observance, described in 1527, survived the reformers. This was the Holy Cross Day procession, with 'mynstralls and myrth of game', in early May to Enmore Green, an important source of Shaftesbury's water, headed by a large trophy known as the Byzant. At the Reformation many such ceremonies were lost, but Shaftesbury's was held more or less continuously from 1364 to 1829, only switching from Sunday to Monday.[11]

In the field of poor relief religious institutions were replaced by secular. The abbey had discharged its duty of providing alms to the poor from an almonry within its 'Broad Hall'. This stood against the market place roughly on the site of the present King Alfred's restaurant. The abbey had also been patron to two quasi-religious foundations in the town. The medieval Hospital of St John the Baptist, which stood in Salisbury Street near Angel Square, and was established for the support of five poor men, was already moribund by 1497, although successive wardens continued to draw a salary for another fifty years. The Magdalen or 'Maudlin' hospital for twelve paupers, in Magdalene Lane west of the abbey precinct, survived the dissolution by a few years, but was ruinous by 1585. The premises were used as a short-lived school from 1625 but then reverted to a poorhouse. On Gold Hill 'Kilpeck's Place', which we encountered earlier being used to endow a chantry, passed following the suppression of chantries to the borough corporation in 1550, and was used for the poor.[12]

How effective the combined benevolence of these institutions may have been in tackling poverty in early Tudor Shaftesbury we cannot know, but it is likely that here, as elsewhere, the town's population was swollen later in the sixteenth century by the arrival of poor, listless vagrants from the surrounding countryside. The corporation took measures to limit this influx, and used the income from borough property to augment poor relief. Individuals too, motivated perhaps by Puritan zeal, established charities, such as Chubb's almshouse for sixteen women, begun in 1611. Its name derives from Matthew Chubb, an unscrupulous and very wealthy Dorchester businessman, who was its principal benefactor. But the idea probably belonged to Margaret and Jane Boden, two daughters of the recorder (or chief executive) of Shaftesbury. Margaret was Matthew Chubb's wife, and a devout Puritan, 'an absolute kind woman and very beneficial to the poor'; Jane had married into the prominent Grove family of Shaftesbury. The almshouse was built in Salisbury Street, and its modern replacement survives, close to a similar but later foundation, 'Spiller's Spital'.[13]

Gerard's next observation, that Shaftesbury was a thoroughfare town much frequented by travellers, is also apparent from other sources. To most of us, grown up with the ring road which carries the main A30 around the town, it is hard to imagine a time when most travellers between London and south-west England would have passed along Salisbury Street and High Street, before struggling down the precipitous Tout Hill to the vale and Sherborne causeway below. The High Street, the mayor stated in a 1620 law suit, 'is a common way as well for carts and carriages as for travellers on horsebacke and on foote from London to the Mount [St Michael's Mount, near Penzance], westwards.' On market days the stalls impeded this traffic and there seems to have been severe congestion.[14]

Traffic, of course, did not arrive only after the abbey had disappeared. The abbey itself, as we have seen, attracted large numbers of pilgrims and tradesmen. And Shaftesbury has always been a nodal point for main roads crossing Wessex in all directions – the town still, it has been noted, has more roads radiating from it than any other in Dorset. What was changing from the sixteenth century was the volume of traffic, especially vehicles, and in time the gradual increase in passing trade more than compensated for the loss of abbey business. Like many other towns in similar roadside positions, innkeeping in Shaftesbury was conducted on a considerable scale, and the names of a dozen establishments operating before 1650 are recorded. Many of these, as well as providing refreshment, would in time become more closely involved in the travel business, offering stabling, horses and carriages for hire, staging posts for coaches, and depots for carriers. A postal service began in 1635, and Shaftesbury became the transfer point for all mail to other Dorset towns; at least two weekly carriers were operating between Shaftesbury and London by 1637; and the first stagecoach ran between London and Exeter through Shaftesbury in 1658.[15]

Gerard's reference to a mayor reminds us of the precarious state of Shaftesbury's local government. The medieval corporation, as we have seen, was subject to the manorial courts of the king and the abbess. As the abbess acquired the majority of properties in the town, she became in effect the sole manorial owner, and with her benign approval the townspeople were allowed a large measure of self-government. But after she had gone the town's right to own property, including common lands and buildings associated with the market, was challenged, and in 1585 all borough property was confiscated by the crown, who sold it to individual entrepreneurs. At the same time the Pembroke family, purchaser of the abbey's estates, began to pursue their claim to rights and dues as manorial owner. The dissolution of the abbey had, in effect, pulled the rug from under the mayor and corporation, and a bitter legal battle, with crippling financial consequences for the town, began. The town secured a charter of incorporation in 1604, but the powers it granted to the corporation were repeatedly and successfully challenged over the next thirty years. Only with the granting of new charters in 1665 and 1684 were the old grievances finally settled.[16]

While it raged, the dispute cost Shaftesbury dear. It was claimed that the town was £200 in debt, and that there were only 30 householders with incomes sufficient to support the 300 people in need. This was doubtless an exaggeration, and in part the natural human tendency to blame society's ills on an individual – in this case a despicable (as the corporation saw it) character named Nicholas Gower who repeatedly challenged their authority; but it must be acknowledged that the shaky foundations of local government in Shaftesbury, as disclosed by the dissolution, hindered the town's development, and especially its ability to cope with the problems faced by many towns during the seventeenth century.[17]

By 'well inhabited' Gerard could mean two things, either that Shaftesbury had a large population, or that it included families of good standing and reputation. No reliable data exist until quite late into the seventeenth century, but then taxation records (of 1664 and 1673) suggest that in Shaftesbury, including the area of St James known as Alcester, there were 365 households, of whom about 100 were too poor to be taxed. This would suggest a total population of between 1,500 and 2,000. Although this may well represent an increase in numbers during the century since the abbey disappeared, Shaftesbury was continuing to slip behind its Dorset rivals. Dorchester (with Fordington) had nearly twice as many families, Poole and Sherborne too were larger, and Weymouth (with Melcombe Regis) and Bridport, were on a par, although Bridport had many more poor families. Within Shaftesbury borough the tax returns (which enumerated the number of hearths in each home) reveal that there were nine households who lived in some affluence, with ten or more hearths, and over thirty with between five and nine hearths.[18]

Some of the more prominent families have left us a reminder of themselves in street names, including the Mustons who ran the *Crown Inn*, and the Haimes, who were millers. Others prospered in the employ of the abbey's successors. John Grove, who gave money to establish a workhouse for the poor,

The Ox House, Bimport.

worked for the Arundells, and probably lived in the Ox House in Bimport. Hardy was aware of this tradition when he called the house 'Old Grove's Place'. Another to do well were the Foyles. John Foyle was born in 1564 into a family who until the dissolution had held abbey land at Hartgrove, south of Shaftesbury. They became tenants of the Arundells, and both John and his brother Robert were employed by Sir Matthew Arundell (who died in 1598) and his successors. John seems to have been an astute land agent and steward, who acquired wealth and position, became prominent in local affairs, and served as MP first for Corfe Castle and then for Shaftesbury itself. In 1620 he bought a manor in Hampshire. His career, from tenant farmer to minor gentry, epitomizes the opportunity for self-aggrandisement offered by the freeing up of monastic lands at the dissolution.[19]

The mural painting by Janet Swiss in Swan's Yard depicts a market in progress during the 1700s in High Street, around the Tudor guildhall in front of St Peter's church.

It is Gerard's final observation about Shaftesbury, its 'plentifull markett', that gives the lie to Hardy's 'general ruin' theory about the dissolution. During the 1560s work was put in hand to pave the town's streets, to erect a butter cross and cistern in the Commons (part of it is now in the Town Museum), and to build a new guildhall. This, replacing a building near the top of Gold Hill, stood in the street outside St. Peter's and was to the familiar west country pattern. The hall itself was at first floor level, supported on five open arches, between which stalls could be erected on market day. The arches appear distinctly medieval, suggesting that they may have been salvaged from the demolished abbey. There were also a fish cross, a covered corn market, butchers' shambles, and numerous stalls which, on market days as we have seen, spilled out on to the highway and obstructed the traffic. A considerable area, extending from the broadening of the High Street (then called Cornhill) near the Mustons Lane junction, westward to envelop the top of Gold Hill and continue around into the Commons where the butter cross stood (by the start of Bell Street) was given over to marketing every Saturday. It was claimed in 1632 that more corn was sold in Shaftesbury market than in any three other Dorset towns put together.[20]

The new guildhall and butter cross, one imagines, were built in a spirit of optimism and renewal, not despair and ruin. And this process of renewal, which began during the decades after the abbey's disappearance and continued for some two centuries, is apparent all over Shaftesbury. It can be seen in the houses climbing Gold Hill, where this chapter began, in Bell Street and Bimport and around Angel Square. There are virtually no medieval buildings left in Shaftesbury, such was the thoroughness of the renewal; but much of the framework of medieval streets and open spaces has been preserved. Not only that – the squared and sometimes carved stonework with which the town was rebuilt should be a constant reminder of its demolished abbey. For there, all around us, it stands.[21]

A stone-lined grave, perhaps of an abbess, excavated in the south transept.

9 On Removing the Rubbish

W HEN THE LAST ABBESS turned to take her last look at the surroundings of her lifetime, that fateful morning in early spring 1539, what she mostly saw was the labour of craftsmen some 450 years earlier. They and their paymasters had expressed an attitude to living, to God and to the material world within which the nunnery operated throughout the middle ages. Individuals held their own views, of course, as they always have, and progress in thought and action had been relentless. The abbey's masonry reflected this – repaired, improved, beautified from time to time. But until 1539 that medieval world remained, foursquare in greensand blocks, delicate in Purbeck columns. When, more than 450 years later, we approach the meagre remains of Shaftesbury Abbey, what we see is the result of later history's attitude to the middle ages – by turns destructive, opportunist, indifferent, curious, fascinated. This chapter is the story of something which, in any substantial sense, has ceased to exist; it is the afterlife of Shaftesbury Abbey.

By no means everything within the abbey precinct was destroyed or changed after 1539. Holy Trinity church remained, and its cemetery was extended southwards to include the 'abbey lytten', the former nuns' burying ground. Many of the utilitarian buildings and workshops lining and running back from the south side of Bimport, on either side of the former abbey gatehouse (the Abbey Walk junction) continued in use and were still standing when a map of Shaftesbury was drawn in 1615. A dovecote survived (on the site

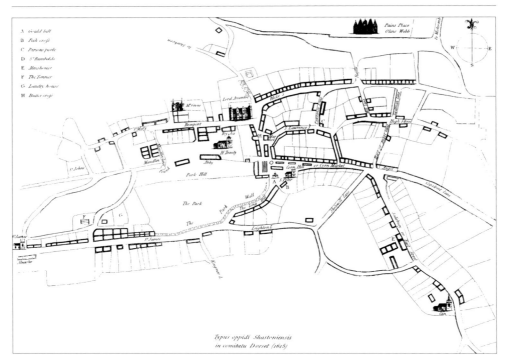

Shaftesbury in 1615, a plan engraved for publication by Hutchins in his history of Dorset.

of the present hospital), and the abbey's 'Broad Hall' facing the market place was also spared – its foundations were discovered during the 1970s in the cellar of the present King Alfred's restaurant. The park, too steep for building, remained. It was described in 1701 as a 'hilly close of meadow' and was also used as a fairground for Welsh cattle. By then gardens, a stable, and a small plot where the stable-owner usually threw the dung, had encroached on it.[1]

What disappeared, and very rapidly (as we saw in chapter 6) was the abbey church with its cloister, chapter house and the convent buildings surrounding it. The buildings were, in the literal Tudor use of the words, 'discovered' and 'defaced' – their lead roofs and squared masonry were removed. The consequences have been graphically described by Laura Sydenham:

> When the site of the abbey church had been exhausted as a quarry for building material, the rubble core of the dismantled walls, exposed to the elements, crumbled and fell, covering the tiled pavements of the church, with the other fragments of masonry and glass, and in time the natural accumulation of dirt and weeds covered all that remained of the once famous church, hiding it from view, and the site became gardens.[2]

On the 1615 map of Shaftesbury a building is shown to the west of the present abbey remains, and is labelled 'Abby'. This is presumably a forerunner of Abbey House, since the present structure incorporates elements of an early-seventeenth century building. By the end of that century the house was in the possession of an old-established Shaftesbury family, the Chamberlaynes, and from 1715 onwards it passed through various hands, mayors and businessmen, and became divided into two. Like much Shaftesbury property the house and its grounds were owned after 1800 for electoral purposes by would-be Parliamentary candidates for the pocket borough, including Robert Dyneley and, from 1818, Lord Grosvenor (later the Marquis of Westminster). The northern portion, known as Abbey Well House, was demolished in 1846 and Lord Westminster replaced it with a school. Both the remaining portion of the school building and Abbey House have salvaged medieval features built into them.[3]

The grounds attached to Abbey House extended both west and east, across the site of the former abbey precinct. To the west, between what is now Abbey Walk and Magdalene Lane, was an area known as the Bowling Green (now the site of Westminster Hospital). To the south and east of the house, covering the church and monastic buildings, was Abbey Green. A map of 1799, precisely drawn, shows the layout of formal gardens across much of the abbey site, with a north–south boundary wall running across it, another wall shielding the gardens from Park Walk, and houses bordering Holy Trinity churchyard. Trees are shown on the site of the present abbey museum and offices. A deed of 1767 suggests that the boundary wall was built then, and that Park Walk was laid out. This fine promenade, tree-lined by 1799, was given to the town by Robert Dyneley in 1816.[4]

Old School House, Abbey Walk,
incorporating a medieval window.

The creation of Park Walk during the later eighteenth century was one manifestation of a growing interest in picturesque landscapes, and in the features of historic and antiquarian interest which could be seen within them. Another was the publication in 1774 of the first edition of a history of Dorset by a local clergyman, John Hutchins, which included a substantial account of Shaftesbury and identified the site of the abbey. Hutchins observed medieval arches within the fabric of Abbey House, recorded that bones and coffins had been found on the abbey site, and described archaeological discoveries (human bones, a ring, and a stone inscribed with the abbey arms) dug up adjacent to the park in 1746 and 1761. These cannot have been the first relics to have been uncovered, but it was only then that anyone thought them worth recording. They represent the first stirrings of curiosity about the lost abbey, and open a new phase in its story.[5]

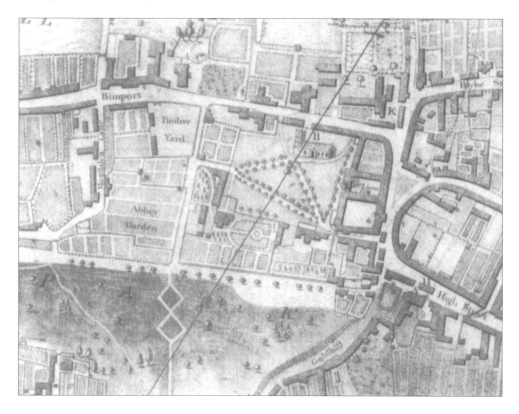

Enlarged detail from William Upjohn's map of Shaftesbury, 1799, showing the area of the former monastic precinct and part of the town (The solid diagonal line is not significant).

Credit for the first deliberate attempt to excavate the site of the abbey must go to Charles Bowles (1766–1837), who in February 1817 communicated the result of his researches on the site (presumably made during the previous year) to the *Gentleman's Magazine*. Bowles sprang from an old Shaftesbury family and had been brought up in the predecessor of the present Barton Hill

Park Walk, looking west. The abbey ruins and museum lie behind the higher portion of the wall to the right. Abbey House (its roof visible) and garden lie beyond.

House, although later in life he lived at Higher Coombe, over the Wiltshire border near Donhead St Mary. He moved easily in the gentry circles of the Shaftesbury area, and served as Lord Grosvenor's land agent as well as recorder (or chief magistrate) for the borough. His brother was the minor but prolific poet, William Lisle Bowles. He helped with the revision of the Shaftesbury portion of Hutchins's history for its second edition, and he was one of a group of historians and antiquarians who associated with and were influenced by Sir Richard Colt Hoare at Stourhead. For Hoare's *History of Modern Wiltshire* he contributed a volume on the hundred of Chalke, which was published in 1830. Hoare's work with William Cunnington in Wiltshire revolutionised the study of archaeology, and doubtless inspired Bowles to examine his own town's principal claim to historical significance.[6]

Mr. URBAN, *Shaftesbury, Feb.* 1.

HAVING obtained permission
from John Dyneley, esq. the
proprietor of the site of the late Abbey
of Shaftesbury, to make any
searches I might think proper, I employed
a workman to dig there, and
at the depth of about six feet from
the surface, came to the floor (as I
apprehend) of the Conventual Church.
It is composed of what is called Roman
tile, having gryphons, dragons,
greyhounds, and other animals, burnt
in the bricks or tiles, interspersed
with the arms of Stourton and Bonham
in painted shields, similarly
burnt in, surrounded in each case
with a border. The bricks or tiles
are about four inches square, and I
send you a Drawing of one *(See
Plate II. fig.* 1), having the arms of
Bonham, done, as I suppose, when
the Abbess Bonham presided — her
Abbacy commenced in 1462; she succeeded
the Abbess Stourton. I met
in the search with many mutilated
Monuments, chiefly of Purbeck marble;
a Drawing also of one of these
I send you *(See Fig.* 2.) It seems as
if those into whose hands the Abbey
materials fell were anxious that the
names of the dead should be concealed,
as the face of the figure is
destroyed, as well as the legend which
once surrounded it. I have met with
several other Monuments, but not a
single one with an inscription. Remains
of the billety mouldings of
massive pillars, of the Purbeck slender
marble shafts, every where dispersed
under-ground, convince me,
that this once grand pile of buildings
was composed of Saxon, Norman,
and the modern architecture or pointed
arch.   CH. BOWLES.

Shaftesbury Abbey's first excavation, communicated by Charles Bowles to the Gentleman's
Magazine *in February 1817.*

Bowles employed a workman to dig on the site, and at a depth of six feet they found ample evidence of the abbey church, in the form of encaustic floor tiles, monuments, and the mouldings of pillars, including slender Purbeck marble shafts. He noted that the faces and inscriptions of the effigies they found were all mutilated, and he concluded that the architecture was Saxon, Norman and 'modern' (by which he meant Gothic). The brief description of their investigations suggests that they were quite wide-ranging, but no plan was published and the whereabouts of any finds (other than the Purbeck effigy, which is in the abbey museum) is unknown. Bowles may have given objects away as souvenirs. Nor is there any suggestion that the work was continued during or after 1817, or that the excavations were left open to view. An architectural historian who visited Shaftesbury nine years later, in 1826, saw nothing to comment on at the site of the abbey, but did report that some monumental slabs and sepulchral effigies found there had been placed in the wall leading down Tout Hill. Since that wall was rebuilt in 1817 it would seem quite likely that they were finds supplied by Bowles from his excavation.[7]

Comparison of the 1799 plan of Shaftesbury with later detailed maps, of 1817, 1845 and 1848, suggests that little change occurred on the site of the abbey church during this period. It straddled the garden of Abbey House, to the west, and that of a house, occupied by Thomas Tucker in 1845, which backed on to Trinity churchyard, to the east. It was presumably in this latter garden that Bowles investigated, and it was certainly here that the next archaeological campaign was waged, in 1861. It was then described as, 'a garden . . . in which there were evident traces of foundations a few feet beneath the surface'.[8]

Around the mid-century Victorian gentlemen interested in antiquities, natural history, folklore and other leisured pursuits formed themselves into local societies and field clubs. Most counties had one or more; Somerset's began in 1849, Wiltshire's in 1853. Dorset started late, not until 1875, and so it was with something of a missionary zeal that the Wiltshire Archaeological and Natural History Society decided to hold its annual meeting for 1861 over the county border in Shaftesbury. One intention, repeatedly mentioned during the affable weekend of speeches, lectures and visits, was to encourage their Dorset hosts to establish their own club.[9]

Before their visit the society had invited James Reynolds, vicar of St Peter's and Holy Trinity, to point out anything worthy of notice, and he asked Lord Westminster's agent, Mr Batten, for permission to dig in the garden and uncover the abbey foundations. Batten and Reynolds began work in July, a few weeks before the society's planned visit, and discovered much of the apsidal east end and chancel aisles of the abbey church. But when they uncovered a grave slab they left it to the Society's experts, in particular Edward Kite, to examine the contents. 'On removing the rubbish', wrote Kite of this excavation, 'a perfect skeleton of a male was discovered, together with the nails and other traces of the wooden coffin in which it had been enclosed.' A pewter chalice found with the burial suggested that the skeleton was that of a priest attached to the abbey. The excavations continued after the Wiltshire society's meeting, and were resumed the following year, since another grave was opened in May 1862. But Kite wrote up his report in June and, at the insistence of Lord Westminster, who was apparently swayed by reverence for the dead, the site was then backfilled.[10]

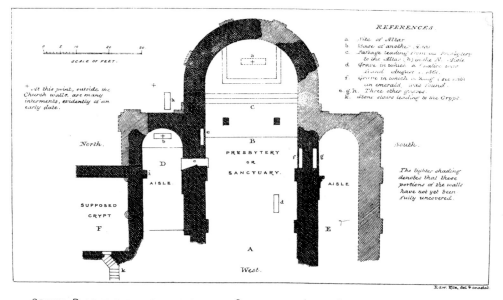

GROUND PLAN OF THE EASTERN PORTION OF SHAFTESBURY ABBEY CHURCH, EXCAVATED IN 1861-2.

Edward Kite's plan of the east end of the abbey church, excavated by Batten and Reynolds in 1861–2, and published in the Wiltshire Archaeological & Natural History Magazine. *The plan is orientated with north to the left.*

We cannot know who was the true inspiration for this programme of excavations. At first glance Reynolds seems to have over-reacted to a simple and obvious request by the meeting's organizer, Kite. But both men had their own agendas. Reynolds seems to have foreseen the need to extend Holy Trinity graveyard, and hoped (by showing that the land to the south was, historically, already consecrated ground) that he might be permitted one day to incorporate it into the churchyard. Kite, a young man of 29 at odds with elderly stalwarts of the Wiltshire society, had become interested in monastic archaeology during building work at Amesbury the previous year, and was probably keen to extend his research to another nunnery. After Shaftesbury his career as an archaeologist failed to develop, although he remained an astute and tenacious historian; following repeated disagreements he was sacked by the society in 1866, and bore a grudge against its ruling élite for most of the rest of his long life – he died in Devizes in 1930 aged 97, still writing historical articles. As for Batten, Lord Westminster's agent, he was an enthusiastic antiquarian who claimed to have been a curator all his life, having investigated ruins in Carthage, Corinth, Egypt and India. He took charge of the temporary museum provided for the society's visit, and exhibited from his own collection a case of humming birds and the tooth of an Asiatic elephant.[11]

For another forty years after 1862, like a giant sleeping under the hill, the abbey was left undisturbed. At least part of the motive for reawakening it in 1902 seems to have been tourism. Shaftesbury in the 1890s, like other old-established market towns ignored by the railway network, found itself losing out to well-connected neighbours, in particular Gillingham; and the borough council was keen to promote a scheme, made possible by legislation in 1896, to bring a light railway (and on it visitors) to the town. A proposal made in March 1902 that the council lease the site and permit a new excavation to uncover the abbey was, therefore, well-timed. Not only was the lease prepared, but a grant of £50 was made to the excavation fund and three councillors were nominated to serve on the fund's committee. The proposal came from Edward Doran Webb, an architect specialising in restoration work, who claimed ancestry from an old Shaftesbury family. He had been a mainstay of archaeological activity in Salisbury during the 1890s, but had converted to Catholicism and moved to Tisbury. His most significant architectural achievement was the Birmingham Oratory.[12]

The lease was finalised on the day ordained for work to begin, 9 June 1902, which was a fortnight before the planned coronation celebrations for Edward VII. The proceedings began with a procession led by the town band, the mayor, aldermen, town clerk, borough surveyor and councillors, to the vicar's garden where they were met by Lord and Lady Stalbridge. Doran Webb handed Lord Stalbridge a crowbar which he drove deeply into the ground and immediately struck the foundations of the abbey. He then turned two spadefuls of earth, before speeches and votes of thanks were made. Excavation work immediately commenced, amid cheers, and after the band had played the national anthem the gathering dispersed.[13]

So grand a publicity stunt was followed by 21 weeks' digging, and a further 22 weeks between May and September 1903. Most of the site available for excavation had by then been uncovered, revealing once more the east end of the abbey church, the choir, choir aisles and crypt. Because the diggers were confined within the area required for total excavation there was nowhere to put the spoil, and much of it was tipped over the escarpment or carted away (thus, incidentally, rendering later backfilling impossible). The council continued to support the work, granting another £50 for the second season and stage-managing a grand event just before Christmas 1903. This was the granting of the freedom of the borough (for the first time ever) to Edward Doran Webb. At the reception, when he was given an inscribed casket with the borough arms engraved in silver, speeches praised him for his dedication, attending every Monday without pay, digging and delving, and 'looking minutely into almost every shovelful of earth'. It was hoped that he would soon be able to pay his visits by train.[14]

In 1904 a third season of excavations was undertaken, but there was a noticeable cooling of enthusiasm. The council failed to stump up its £50 grant, leaving the excavation fund £52 in debt at the end of the year. Receipts from casual visitors to the site were down on 1903, despite two organized society visits. The diggers excavated part of the abbey cloister, but were unable to work on the nave of the church or the western ends of the transepts because these lay beyond the site boundary, in Abbey House garden. To enable them to do this the council, in April, agreed to take a lease on Abbey House. But then, despite Doran Webb's plea to be allowed time to excavate in the garden, they let it to a tenant who appears to have denied the archaeologists access. In any case, with

Shaftesbury Abbey Excavation Fund.

THIRD REPORT.

The Hon. Director of the Shaftesbury Abbey Excavation Fund has pleasure in submitting the following Report on the work carried out under his direction during the summer of 1904.

ON Monday, the sixth of June, 1904, the workmen commenced removing the earth from the site of the Cloister, which stood on the south side of the nave of the Church, completing the work, including laying the Cloister-garth with turf by the end of the first week in November.

The sum of one hundred pounds has been paid this year for labour alone; photography and printing, including the publishing of the report for 1903, with the lithograph plan of the Church, and making the block for the cover, has cost ten pounds eleven shillings and eleven pence; whilst the putting up of a wooden fence across the ground to divide it from the garden of the Abbey House, and sundry other small accounts have brought up the total of the amount expended this year to one hundred and thirty-nine pounds thirteen shillings and eleven pence.

But although, as will be seen by comparing the Hon. Treasurer's Balance Sheet for 1902 and 1903 with the one for the present year, the expenses have been much less. On the other hand the receipts from donations show a great falling off, and unless this can by some means or another be remedied it is difficult to see how the work can be carried to a successful issue.

Part of Doran Webb's pessimistic report following the 1904 season of excavations.

the debt unresolved, there was no question of a 1905 season and the excavations came to an end.[15]

There was no ostensible rift between Doran Webb and the council. He was guest of honour at the mayoral banquet in November 1904, when he gave the council a loving cup, and again in November 1905, when the hope was expressed that he would one day serve as mayor. In 1908, wearing his architect's hat, he designed a new chancel for Holy Trinity church. But little more was seen of him in Shaftesbury, although he lived on at Tisbury for many years, dying in 1931. No railway ever came to the town. And nothing more was done to the site, which could not easily be backfilled, and so became overgrown and damaged by frost. Curious visitors could pay a shilling, obtain the key and inspect the site; one in 1909 apparently wrote in the comments column of the visitors' book, 'What is there to comment upon?'[16]

As the tenancy of Abbey House was due to end in 1911 the council began to act. A letter to Doran Webb in August 1910 seems not to have resulted in the hoped-for meeting to discuss the site's future. In June 1911 the council adopted an ambitious plan which included making a bowling green on part of the site and relocating the bandstand to within the excavated area. They also wrote again to Doran Webb to remind him of his undertaking to erect a shed on the site to store the archaeological finds. But nothing could be done without the moribund excavation fund committee's approval. In desperation the town clerk wrote to its treasurer in May 1913, and was advised simply to take possession of the site, at the same time handing over the balance of the fund, about £7. As new custodians of the site the council did not proceed with the bandstand and bowling green, but did erect a shed. Partly, no doubt, this was to release space in the town hall occupied ever since the excavations by the finds; but it was also prompted by another impending visit from the Wiltshire Archaeological and Natural History Society, planned for July 1914. The council just met their deadline, as is clear from the account of the visit:

> From the church the party proceeded to the site of the abbey excavations, where the Vicar again very kindly gave an account of such remains of walls as are visible, most of them rapidly crumbling away, and showed with justifiable satisfaction the new wooden museum shed, which had only been finished that day in readiness for the Society's visit. . .[17]

There is a sad repetitiveness about the history of Shaftesbury Abbey through much of the twentieth century. New owners and enthusiasts have come and gone, each re-excavating parts of the site and criticising their predecessors' lack of expertise or care. After Shaftesbury council took responsibility of the site in 1913 it seems to have been neglected once more. As a property of Lord Stalbridge it was included in the sequence of sales of his Shaftesbury estate which followed the war, in 1918–19, and its new owner was Robert Borley. In 1921, waiving the usual entrance fee, he and Doran Webb showed members of the Dorset Natural History and Antiquarian Field Club around the site. Doran Webb recalled that he had hoped that the site would have been taken over by a larger body than his excavation committee and made a national matter. Borley, who had taken possession less than four months earlier, deplored the present neglected state of the site, 'which is due entirely to the lack of interest and care shown by the previous owners, the corporation'. He hoped before long to improve matters. Concerned local residents, however, suspected that he planned to build on the site, and they were successful in having it designated a scheduled ancient monument in 1924.

The Dorset Field Club met there again in 1929, when ownership had passed to Rev S. F. Hancock. He showed them the results of his own excavations on the site, and described his plans to preserve what remained of the flooring, by covering it with Shaftesbury town grit. But Hancock died in 1930, and Abbey House and the excavation site were offered to Shaftesbury council for £3,000. They declined to purchase them, and they were sold to Mrs Frances Claridge, of a local firm of estate agents, whose son – with more bravado than expertise – immediately began his own campaign of excavations.[18]

The work of John Wilson Claridge, conducted between 1930 and 1932, was more extensive than most, and included not only the find of the supposed relics of St Edward, described in chapter 3, but also the first investigation of much of the nave. Although Claridge took the credit much of the hard work was done by his employee, Bert Richards, a builder who had previously worked at the abbey for the Rev. Hancock. Richards was also responsible for the abbey lodge building, the shrine for St Edward's relics, and the boundary wall against Holy Trinity churchyard. Claridge was a great self-publicist, reawakening popular interest in the abbey for the first time since Doran Webb in 1902–3, and

View of the crossing, chancel and south transept, with the 1930s Abbey Lodge beyond.

in 1931 he opened a small museum of finds (with Bert as curator). He was also a responsible excavator to the extent that he published a report of his work. But by 1932 the Claridges were trying to sell the site, and enlisted the council's help in interesting a national body such as the Office of Works, the Society for the Protection of Ancient Buildings or the National Trust. None took up the offer, and the Claridges remained until 1951, running the ruins as a business. In their last year of trading, 1950, they claimed to have admitted 5,000 visitors during the five summer months.[19]

The site was put up for auction in 1951 but failed to sell. Soon afterwards it was purchased by Laura Sydenham and Phyllis Carter who, with the help of an archaeological surveyor, began to restore and re-excavate the site, which (in Sydenham's words) had been shamefully neglected once more. They discovered earlier work beneath the Norman foundations at the east end, and revealed a late-medieval tomb recess in the presbytery. But Sydenham's main achievements lay in clearing and laying out the gardens, creating a museum of finds, and writing the first full-scale history of the abbey, which was published in 1959.[20]

Laura Sydenham died before 1968, when the four-headed finial was erected on Abbey Lodge to her memory, and her friend Phyllis Carter continued to own and manage the site until her own death in September 1979. During

Carter's time, in 1971, a detailed survey of the ruins was undertaken by the Royal Commission on Historical Monuments; it was published in 1972. After her death an ambitious plan to form a trust and buy both the abbey ruins and Holy Trinity church (by then redundant) foundered, and the site passed again into private hands. It remained open to the public during the summer months until 1984, but failed to reopen in 1985. A company, the Shaftesbury Abbey and Museum Trust, was incorporated under the aegis of the county, district and town authorities, to acquire the site (for £82,000), which it did in January 1986. A salaried curator was appointed, and management of the trust was assumed by a body of Friends of Shaftesbury Abbey, formed the next year. In 1988 the Trust and Friends celebrated in style the 1,100th anniversary of the abbey's founding, and in 1995 a new altar was consecrated. This is carved with the name of Edward, king and martyr, and

The new buildings incorporating museum, shop and office, a drawing by Frank Garbutt.

has an inner compartment reserved for his relics, should they ever return to Shaftesbury. During the 1990s small-scale archaeological investigations and surveys have been undertaken by professional archaeologists within the site and in the vicinity. But the principal concern has been with the interpretation of the abbey's history and archaeology by means of an entirely new museum. After years of planning and discussion an offer of part-funding by the Heritage Lottery Fund was confirmed in October 1997, and the museum was opened (by the television presenter Julian Richards, who lives nearby) in May 1999.[21]

Official opening of the new museum and facilities in May 1999.

Nothing we do now can undo the damage caused to Shaftesbury Abbey by those earlier attitudes – destructive, opportunist, indifferent, curious, or fascinated. But we can at least ensure that the abbey has an afterlife, and that it will continue to be remembered and appreciated for the remarkable monument that it once was.

10 The Reality Now – A Guide

SHAFTESBURY ABBEY MUSEUM AND GARDEN are open throughout the summer months, from April to October, and a guide booklet and audio tour are available to assist visitors in exploring the fragmentary remains of the abbey church and part of the cloister which are open to view within the garden. The pleasures and sensations to be derived on a warm afternoon from strolling in this peaceful enclave are beyond the scope of this history. The purpose of this chapter is more prosaic. It is to complement the experience of visiting the museum and garden by taking a tour around other parts of Shaftesbury, to search for what remains of the world the nuns inhabited, and to see how a dead abbey continues to influence a living town.*

The tour begins and ends at the entrance gate to the museum and garden in Park Walk. In the following pages directions are given in paragraphs of italic type, and the descriptions in numbered paragraphs of normal type relate to the numbers on the accompanying sketch map. Where appropriate cross-references are made to other chapters in this book.

Stand in Park Walk facing the museum and garden entrance.

---

* Note: The opening period and provision of guides relate to the year in which this book was published (2003) and may change over time.

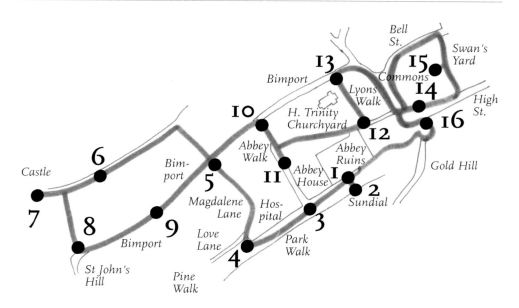

1 You are confronted by a long stone wall with, to the right of the entrance, the abbey lodge built in the 1930s (see p. 127) and surmounted by a four-faced finial commemorating the abbey's owner until her death in 1968, Laura Sydenham (p. 128). The abbey garden extends to the right as far as the lodge gate, and to the left as far as the end of the raised elevation of walling. Behind this wall is the modern museum, opened in 1999 (pp. 129–30). In the garden, which runs back to the edge of Holy Trinity churchyard (you can see the church tower beyond), are all the features that remain exposed of the abbey church. The ruins comprise principally the footings of the exterior walls, the bases of columns forming the nave arcade and the crossing, the crypt adjoining the north transept, excavated burial vaults and portions of tiled floors (pp. 42–4, 49–51). Other structures include a medieval cross from the town, reset on the site of the high altar and, in the chancel, a modern stone altar. There is also a shrine built during the 1930s to house the supposed relics of St Edward (pp. 37–9). The church is roughly in line with the wall on to Park Walk, so that its east end lies behind the abbey lodge, and its west end (which has never been excavated) just beyond the end of the higher section of walling away to your left, in the garden of Abbey House.

Park Walk was laid out as a fashionable promenade in the eighteenth century, and the wall cuts right across the abbey precinct (p. 117). The cloister lay to the south of the church, adjoining its nave, and extended across what has become Park Walk, in the area to the left of where you are standing. Part of its footings remain in the garden beyond the wall. The cloister was probably a square of 33 yards (about 30 metres), with buildings ranged along its sides. The abbey refectory and kitchen occupied the south range, with their backs close up to the edge of the promontory. They have not been excavated (pp. 53–4).

Turn around and walk through the gate to the edge of the promontory, where there are two seats and the golden jubilee sundial.

2 This stunning view across Blackmore Vale to the distant chalk hills beyond Blandford and Sturminster Newton includes several medieval estates which belonged to Shaftesbury Abbey. Melbury Beacon, the prominent hill in front of you, forms part of an escarpment running south, beneath which sits a string of the abbey's villages – Melbury Abbas, Fontmell Magna, Compton Abbas and Iwerne Minster. Other possessions lay in the valley floor further to the right of the view (see map p. 20). Dropping sharply away beneath you is the abbey's park, which is confined by the medieval line of St James's Street, the suburb of houses at its foot. This culminates in St James's church, away to your right. Beyond this suburb lay the abbey's fishponds, and to the left, out of sight, runs the massive wall which forms one side of Gold Hill. When excavations took place on the site of the abbey church during the period 1902–4 much of the spoil was tipped over the precipice here (p. 124).

Return to Park Walk, turn left and follow the wall away from the town as far as the war memorial in the form of a Celtic cross.

3 All this area lay within the abbey precinct. It probably accommodated the abbess's lodging and perhaps the infirmary (pp. 53–4). Behind the wall to your right is Abbey House, which was built in the seventeenth century but includes much stonework from the medieval abbey (p. 117). The war memorial cross stands opposite one end of Abbey Walk. At the further end of this lane was the main entrance to the precinct, the abbey gatehouse (p. 56), and we shall encounter its site presently. Beyond Abbey Walk is the Westminster Hospital, a

Victorian foundation much altered and expanded, and somewhere close to its octagonal extension must be the site of the abbey dovecot or pigeon house (p. 57).

Continue in the same direction past the public shelter as far as the end of the low wall enclosing the hospital extension.

4 At this point a path (Stoney Path) begins to diverge down the slope to the left. This led to the abbey laundry house behind St James's Street (p. 57). Straight ahead the tree-lined path (Pine Walk) must represent the position of the earthen defences along the south side of King Alfred's original Saxon town or burh, established in about 880; and beyond the low wall to the right Love Lane is probably the successor to an early road which ran along inside the defences (pp. 10, 12).

Turn to the right and slightly back, and go through the kissing gate into Love Lane. Turn right and follow the lane round the bend (where it becomes Magdalene Lane) past the entrance to Westminster Hospital on your right. Continue to the end of Magdalene Lane, where it emerges on to the road called Bimport.

5 You have been walking along the eastern edge of the original Saxon town, where it abuts the abbey precinct. The town was to your left, the precinct to your right (see map, p. 8). And you have arrived at about the point where there would have been an entrance from the east (your right) into the town. This is probably what Asser, Alfred's biographer, meant when he wrote that the abbey was established next to the east gate of Shaftesbury (see p. 144 note 12, where alternatives are also discussed). Near this entrance, too, stood one of the town's medieval churches, dedicated to St Mary, but this had gone before 1500. Magdalene Lane takes its name from an almshouse, the Magdalen or Maudlin Hospital, which occupied a site behind you and to your left from the fourteenth through to the seventeenth century. Bimport (meaning 'within the *port* or town') is so-called because it led into the Saxon town and formed the main street through its centre. There is another street with this unusual name in Malmesbury, which has similar Saxon origins (p. 10).

Cross Bimport (with care) and continue in the same direction along the driveway opposite. This becomes a path with an open grassed area to your left and railings ahead of you. Follow the path around to your left and stroll along as far as the viewpoint marker.

6 You have now completed the eastern flank of the Saxon town and have walked about halfway along the northern defences, which are protected by the steep slope of the promontory. The grassed area to your left has probably always been open land since the inhabitants of the first Shaftesbury decided to move further east to colonize the site of the present town. This process seems to have been under way by the eleventh century (pp. 25–7). Consequently this area is now protected from modern development because of the likely wealth of archaeological remains beneath it.

The panoramic view across the countryside north of Shaftesbury is just as spectacular as that to the south where our tour began. Much of the distant view towards the right lies in Wiltshire, including the wooded hillslope (Kingsettle Hill) nearby on the right. Beyond this hill, in the Vale of Wardour, lay some of the abbey's largest and most lucrative estates, the Donheads and Tisbury (see map, p. 20). Somerset lies in the far distance towards the left, its boundary marked by the wooded ridge of Selwood Forest (look for Alfred's Tower, erected in the eighteenth century to commemorate the victory in 878 after which Alfred built abbeys at Athelney and Shaftesbury). The large, relatively flat area in the middle distance, surrounding the town of Gillingham (you can easily pick out its industrial estate) was in the middle ages the royal forest of Gillingham, from which the king allowed the abbey servants to collect firewood for the community every day (p. 69). And in the foreground, at the foot of the hill, is the suburb of Enmore Green, the principal source of water for the medieval town and abbey.

Continue along the tarmac path to the far corner, where it turns left, and (optionally, since this stretch may be muddy) go through the kissing gate at the corner and walk on about 70 metres.

7 From here (and also from the gate) you can make out an area of rough, broken ground to the left. This is the site of the twelfth-century castle, built at the far corner of the promontory (p. 26). The castle site would have been beyond the limit of the Saxon town, since its defences must have turned southward somewhere near here.

Retrace your steps to the gate and follow the tarmac path alongside the high fence until you reach Bimport. Please supervise dogs and children, as the path ends in a busy road with no pavement.

8 To your right you can see that Bimport is coming to an end, and that it continues around a right-angled corner as St John's Hill. This street leads to the exit from the Saxon town at the south-western corner of its defences, and then off the hill to St James suburb. It is named from a parish church of St John, which lay around the corner close to a town gate, and fell out of use in the sixteenth century (p. 12). An ancient spreading yew tree remains in its overgrown former churchyard. Looking left along Bimport you can see on the opposite side a long range of greensand cottages, with five chimneys. This is now called Edwardstow, and is the only example of domestic architecture in Shaftesbury to retain substantial medieval work. It dates from about 1500, and so would have existed before the abbey was demolished (p. 30).

Turn left and walk along Bimport, negotiating the busy, narrow road with great care. Pause when you reach a turning (Langfords Lane) on your right.

9 You have been walking along the main street bisecting the Saxon town, the spine road from which the town's properties ran back at right angles. Although the houses are much newer, their property boundaries in many cases probably reflect those laid out in the ninth century when the town was planned. At Langfords Lane (which follows one such boundary) you will notice that Bimport changes direction slightly and broadens. This is probably to accommodate the original street market of the town.

Continue along Bimport, past Magdalene Lane (where you crossed earlier) until you reach the next turning on your right, Abbey Walk.

10 At the Magdalene Lane junction you left the Saxon town by its east gate and have been following the edge of the abbey precinct on your right. During the abbey's existence this Bimport frontage would have been lined with storage buildings, including a granary, woolhouse and larderhouse; and behind them were courtyards occupied and surrounded by other functional buildings, including a malthouse, brewery and wellhouse (pp. 56–7). Evidence for this industrial activity was found by archaeologists when an extension to the hospital car park was built in this area in 1996. The opposite side of Bimport lay beyond the precinct boundary, and here substantial gentry houses were built in the sixteenth and seventeenth centuries (pp. 111–12). The Ox House, although much altered, is a surviving example, and was used as the setting for an incident in Hardy's *Jude the Obscure*.

The Abbey Walk turning is on the site of the abbey gatehouse, the principal entrance for visitors to the whole monastic complex. It may have been quite an impressive structure, capable of accommodating distinguished (including royal) guests. Beyond it, lining Bimport, were further abbey buildings, including stores, stabling and offices.

Turn right along Abbey Walk, noticing the buildings of King Edward's Court on your left. Continue towards the war memorial, but stop when you reach Old School House on your left.

11 The suite of Victorian buildings now known as King Edward's Court belongs to a former primary school, which is celebrated as the scene of an episode in Hardy's novel, *Jude the Obscure*. They occupy the site, and probably respect the external boundaries, of a series of three linked courtyards around which were ranged important abbey buildings (see plan, p. 54). These were the offices or chambers for the sacristan (responsible for all the equipment used in church services), and the steward (responsible for the abbey's estates). Here too were the exchequer or treasury, accommodation for guests, and a suite of rooms where the novices lived and studied. Old School House, which lies beyond the site of these courtyards, is a mid-nineteenth century school, but you can see that a medieval window (of about 1500) has been incorporated into its structure. Although from its position this might be assumed to have come from the abbey, it is perhaps more likely to be a relic from Holy Trinity church, salvaged when the church was rebuilt during the 1840s (p. 117). Behind this house and to its right you can see the much larger Abbey House, whose entrance gate is nearby.

Retrace your steps along Abbey Walk past Abbey Court and turn right along the short lane which leads into Holy Trinity churchyard. At the gate take the right of the two avenues of pollarded trees, which leads diagonally across the churchyard to its far corner, where there is a gateway.

12 Holy Trinity is a Victorian rebuilding (1840–2) of a church which began life as a chapel within the monastic precinct, and was later granted the status of a parish church. It is no longer in religious use. A new chancel was provided for it in 1908, and this was designed by Edward Doran Webb, who also excavated the abbey ruins between 1902 and 1904 (pp. 123–6). The ruins lie directly beyond the churchyard wall to the right of the avenue, behind the yew trees. The churchyard was in the middle ages the nuns' cemetery.

The gateway leads out to the corner of two narrow lanes, Church Lane in front of you, Lyons Walk to your left. Walk left along Lyons Walk until it emerges into Bimport. Look out for traffic using this narrow portion of Bimport.

13 Lyons Walk, so called because it ran behind a former inn, the *Red Lion* (rebuilt in the 1820s as the *Grosvenor*), marks the boundary between the monastic precinct and the medieval town. Standing at its Bimport end you are facing a plot (from the Old Rectory to the corner) which was chosen by the Arundell family for their mansion house. Thomas Arundell, who acquired the abbey site at its dissolution, preferred not to adapt existing monastic buildings to make a house, but instead razed most of it to the ground and built instead a 'fair turreted house' here. Parts of it remained until the nineteenth century (p. 99).

Turn right along Bimport, and right again at the corner. The road opens out into a wide area, The Commons. Keep on the pavement past the Grosvenor Hotel and Church Lane where you reach the zebra crossing. Cross and continue in the same direction along High Street for about 25 metres until you are standing opposite the town hall, which is across the street on your right.

14 You have now left the abbey precinct and walked into the centre of the town which was established here (in preference to the Saxon town on the promontory) from the eleventh century, and which flourished outside the wealthy abbey's walls. Until the modern ring road was built the High Street formed part of the main road from London to Exeter and Cornwall, and at times would have been thronged with travellers (p. 109). The broadening of the street at The Commons (opposite the *Grosvenor Hotel*) and here at the corner of High Street by the town hall enabled stalls to be erected and flourishing markets to take place (pp. 112–13). After the dissolution of the abbey, during the 1560s, a butter cross and cistern were built in The Commons, and a guildhall or market house on columns in front of St Peter's church. This area was then known as Cornhill. St Peter's church (opposite you, to the left of the town hall) was and is the principal place of Anglican worship for the town (pp. 107–8). The present building dates mostly from the decades around 1500. The town hall dates from 1826–7, with additions (the clock tower and porch) made in 1879. If you look back towards the zebra crossing you will see a mock timber-framed building, King Alfred's. This is on part of the site of the abbey's Broad Hall, from where alms were dispensed to the town's poor (p.55).

Continue along High Street, past Lloyds Bank, and turn left into Swan's Yard. As you turn glance across the street to the gable above Squires's outfitter's shop, where you will see a stone carved with the abbey's coat of arms. About halfway along Swan's Yard turn to your left to find a modern mural painting.

15 The mural, by Janet Swiss, was created in 2002 and depicts the centre of Shaftesbury (close to where you have just been standing) as it might have looked in the 1700s, including the Tudor guildhall in front of St Peter's church. Swan's Yard occupies two medieval burgage plots, one running north from High Street to meet another running south from Bell Street. Long rectangular plots such as these are characteristic of most Saxon and medieval towns, and suggest that areas of the town were deliberately planned. It is very common for medieval property boundaries to survive even when all the standing buildings that occupy them (as in Shaftesbury) are later. Look to the top of Swan's Yard. The building in Bell Street opposite, a Methodist chapel, is on the site of one of the town's many parish churches, St Laurence's, and Bell Street in the middle ages was known as St Laurence's Street.

Continue to the top of Swan's Yard and turn left into Bell Street. Follow the pavement around The Commons, opposite the Grosvenor Hotel, until you reach the zebra crossing again. Cross and turn left, following round in front of the town hall. Descend with care the narrow cobbled path between the town hall and St Peter's church beyond.

16 As you make your way down this path you will see above you the Sun and Moon sign of a former inn. This building is on the site of 'Kilpeck's Place' (pp. 105–6), and at one time the property extended beneath the church to incorporate part of its crypt. The path opens out behind the town hall into a famous view, of cottages climbing down the left side of a steep cobbled hill (Gold Hill), and facing a massive masonry wall on the right. Try, in adjusting to this scene, to imagine it without the town hall behind you (which is a relatively late intrusion), and to visualize medieval peasants and tradesmen toiling up from Blackmore Vale below to where Gold Hill at its top would have broadened and funnelled out into the market place (picture p. 58). There was a market cross in this area, next to the stocks (p. 101); and the original town guildhall stood in the middle ages at the top of the great wall, now the first cottage in Park Lane. The wall itself is the only substantial remains in Shaftesbury of the medieval abbey complex. Much of it dates from the fourteenth and fifteenth centuries, and it defined the edge of the abbey's property, its sloping park which lies beyond.

You could end your tour here, with a visit to the town museum on your left, or return to the abbey ruins entrance. To do this take the narrow path, Park Lane, on your right (as you look down Gold Hill). It opens out into Park Walk, where you began.

17 Although Shaftesbury Abbey's fine buildings were all swept away at or soon after its sixteenth-century dissolution, medieval properties which were built and owned by the abbey remain elsewhere. Notable among them are Place Farm and barn at Tisbury (not open to the public), the so-called tithe barn and related buildings at Bradford on Avon, and the Saxon church of St Lawrence, also in Bradford on Avon. These and other survivors are discussed on pp. 86–8.

*The Purbeck effigy discovered by Bowles in 1816 (see
p. 120), now in the Abbey Museum.*

Notes

1 PALADORE

[1] Barnes 1879, 427 (*Shaftesbury Feair*);
Hardy 1895, 249. The name and legends
probably originate with Geoffrey of
Monmouth, writing in the twelfth century:
see Thorpe 1966, 80; Gerard 1980, 89–90.
Etymology: Mills 1989, 142–3.
[2] Dorset SMR ST82SE 169, 173. Note that
hitherto unrecognised hillforts have recently
been identified on the sites of two Wiltshire
towns, Ludgershall and Malmesbury: Ellis
2000, 100–1; *WANHM* 94 (2001), 249. The
likelihood that Shaftesbury was a hillfort was
discussed as long ago as 1893: Mayo 1894,
36–7.
[3] Keen 1999, 1 and 12 (note 2), retracting
his earlier suggestion in Keen 1984, 212–13,
221. A second *byrig* name, Boltbury, was
recorded by Hutchins (1868, 40) and
reiterated by Mayo (1894, 36–7); see also
Mills 1989, 154.
[4] Hall 2000, 12, 15, 17–19, 35. Tisbury's
minster status is an assumption based on
early references to a monastery there and
consideration of its position within the
medieval hundred of Dunworth.
[5] The maps by Hall (2000, 12–18) are
useful for boundaries. Enmore Green (the
name means 'duck–pond') was supplying

Shaftesbury's water 'time out of mind' before
the 1520s: Hutchins 1868, 629. Rutter
(1990) offers a possible solution to the brief
boundary clauses of the Saxon charter. For
the charter, and discussion, see Kelly 1996,
93–4 (no.22).
[6] This summary draws on the excellent
paper by Keynes (1999), especially pp. 18–37.
A rather different picture is painted by Smyth
1995, which is countered by Keynes 1996.
[7] Recent research on the *Burghal Hidage*
is brought together in Hill and Rumble 1996;
see especially pp. 106–7, 216–17. See also
Slater 2000, 590–1.
[8] Hill and Rumble 1996; Keen 1984, 231;
Keynes 1999, 38. The problematic reference
to *Cissanbyrig* or *Tissanbyrig* in the list was
identified by Brooks (1964, 75–9) as
Chisbury near Great Bedwyn in eastern
Wiltshire, and this has been accepted by
most later commentators. Crowley, however
(1987, 197) prefers the older identification,
with Tisbury; if this is correct, Shaftesbury
would not, presumably, have had any
responsibility for south Wiltshire. For
Lydford see below, note 12.
[9] Biddle 1976, 126. I owe the suggestion
that the scheme may not have been
completed to Douglas Crowley. In this case
Shaftesbury and Tisbury might have been

alternatives for burghal status.

¹⁰ The inscription is discussed in detail by RCHM 1972, 57, and Murphy 1994, 45. Okasha (1983, 98) is unconvinced by the identification. For William of Malmesbury's account see Smith 1991, especially p. 12.

¹¹ Keynes 1999, 39. John Leland, visiting in c.1544, reported that the stone had stood in St Mary's chapel at the town's end, which had by then been demolished: Smith 1910, 110–11. Leland's belief that Alfred refounded an earlier nunnery (based on a lost inscription) is explained by Murphy 1994, 41.

¹² Hill and Rumble 1996, 216–17 and note 69. Magdalene Lane: RCHM 1972, 75. Lydford: Biddle 1976, 131–2; Haslam 1984a, 256–9. The site of the *burh's* defences suggested in this and subsequent paragraphs agrees with RCHM (1972, 75; and Rutter 1986, 19–20), but is not the one adopted by most recent commentators (Keen 1984, 232–3; Murphy 1992, 30; Keynes 1999, 39), who favour a line further east which could embrace the abbey. But if the *burh* was planned some years before the abbey why should provision have been made for a large monastic precinct within it? And does not Asser's expression *iuxta orientalem portam* more naturally imply an extra–mural development? At both Wilton and Christchurch (Twynham) there is no indication that burghal defences extended around their respective abbeys, although in both cases water offered a natural defence. A counter–argument that Alfred may have intended to found the abbey some years before 888 has been proposed (by Elinor Murphy, to whom I am indebted for discussing this point), based on the fact that Pope Marinus sent Alfred relics of the Holy Cross in 884. These may have been intended for Shaftesbury, where the Holy Rood was later venerated (noted by Whitelock 1930,

169–70). But 884 is still later than the suggested founding of the town.

¹³ Bimport: Mills 1989, 145. Intra–mural or 'wall' streets: Biddle 1976, 130–1, and examples in Haslam 1984a, *passim*. St Mary's and St John's: Penn 1980, 85, 87. Churches at Saxon entrances: Morris 1989, 214–22.

¹⁴ Keynes and Lapidge 1983, 25–37; Keynes 1999, 32–7. Dumville (1992, 185–205) describes Alfred's religious reforms and demonstrates how they were continued by his successors.

¹⁵ Good discussions of this large subject can be found in Morris 1989, 93–139; and Aston 2000, 29–62.

¹⁶ Keynes and Lapidge 1983, 102–5; Keynes 1999, 17–18. Elinor Murphy's exhaustive research on the question of the foundation date concludes that it took place between 887 and 889 (Murphy 1994, 50).

¹⁷ Hill 1967; Keynes 1993, 155.

¹⁸ Dutton 1988, 141 places Egbert's Stone at Shaftesbury, but this is rejected by Keynes 1999, 60–1, note 16. Penselwood, Stourton (hence Alfred's Tower) and Kingston Deverill are among other suggested locations, but the site has never been satisfactorily demonstrated.

¹⁹ Keynes 1999, 30, 39–40

2 A GROUP OF NOBLE DAMES

¹ Keynes and Lapidge 1983, 105, translating *habitationi sanctimonialium habile*.

² Gilchrist 1994, 25–32, who includes lists and distribution maps. She includes also possible double houses at Bath and Malmesbury, but both rely on slender evidence and were in any case under Hwiccian or Mercian control at the time.

[3] Yorke 1989, 97, 103–5.

[4] Summarised in Yorke 1995, 206–7; Gilchrist 1994, 32–3 (both with distribution maps; Meyer 1981, 334–5. See also Coldicott 1989, chapter 2, and Foot 2000a, 162–5. Cnut: Keynes 1999, 55.

[5] I have conflated Asser's two references to Aethelgifu: Keynes and Lapidge 1983, 90, 105. She is fully discussed by Murphy 1994, 43–4, and Keynes 1999, 40–1. Meyer (1981, 333 note 3) includes her in a list of venerated Wessex royal women, but offers no evidence. She has probably become confused with Aelfgifu: see Ridyard 1988, 170.

[6] Keynes 1999, 45–6; Smith 1991, 4, 6, 12–13.

[7] Wynflaed: Keynes 1999, 43–5; Foot 2000a, 136–9. It is possible that a namesake of this Wynflaed was also associated with Shaftesbury. She left an impressive wardrobe, which is described in her will: see Owen 1979. Eadgifu: Kelly 1996, xiii; Foot 2000a, 181–3. Vowesses: Yorke 1989, 101, 108–9; Gilchrist 1994, 34–5. Abbesses: Knowles 1972, 219. Benefactresses: Kelly 1996, xxvii. In general see Meyer 1981.

[8] Yorke 1989, 105–11; Yorke 1995, 218–20; Meyer 1977, 51–61; Dumville 1992, 198–205.

[9] Meyer 1981, 341–2; Keynes and Lapidge 1983, 105; Kelly 1996, xxiii–xxiv, and charters 7 and 21.

[10] Kelly 1996, xxii–xxvii; and see discussions in chapters 3 and 6.

[11] RCHM 1972, 58, 60, 61; Rutter 2003; Keynes and Lapidge 1983, 105–7.

[12] The significance of William's description of Athelney is discussed by Hinton 1977, 41–2 and Aston 2000, 63–6, who illustrates the St Gall plan. See also Murphy 1994, 48 for a possible stonebuilt successor at Athelney.

[13] Scobie and Qualmann 1993; Coldicott 1989, 3, 5, 11–12.

[14] Scott 1996, 26–43; Scott 2001, 155–6; see also Coldicott 1989, 6–15; Collier 1990.

[15] Murphy (1994, 45–6) discusses the relic of the True Cross; Rutter (2003) argues for the possibility that Shaftesbury had a crypt.

[16] Ridyard 1988, 170–1, discussed below, chapter 3. See also Gem 1978, 109–10.

[17] Saxon charter: Rutter 1990 (see also chapter 1, note 5); Domesday: discussed in Penn 1980, 85; William's remark: Smith 1991, 4, 12.

[18] Smith 1956, 257–63 discusses the various nuances of *vicus* and its English equivalent, wick.

[19] Shaftesbury churches and parishes: Penn 1980, 85. Saxon churches in towns: Morris 1989, ch. 5; Schofield and Vince 1994, ch. 6. The possible Saxon origins of St Rumbold's, (in Salisbury Street) are discussed in SDAG 1991, 41, where Warwick Rodwell suggests that the dedication is eleventh century and the church relates to a late Saxon suburban expansion. Late–Saxon pottery has been found on the site of St Peter's: Keen 1980.

3 EDWARDSTOW

[1] Domesday: see Kelly 1996, xv, n.10; William of Malmesbury: Smith 1991, 14; parallels: Fell 1978, 5–6; medieval forms and discussion: Mills 1989, 141, 142–3.

[2] Fryde *et al* 1986, 27

[3] Yorke 1999, 103–6; Stafford 1978, 21–4; MacDonald 2000, 19–22.

[4] Garmonsway 1953, 123, 125; Ridyard 1988, 44–7, 163. A recent popular discussion of the sources for the murder is in MacDonald 2000, 23–7.

[5] Adapted and summarized from the Latin text edited by Raine (1879, 448–51),

omitting the hagiographical elements. The date and contents are discussed by Ridyard (1988, 47–8).

6 Fell 1971, xx (authorship); the murder is described *ibid*, 4–6. See also Ridyard 1988, 48–9; Yorke 1999, 99–102. Fell (1978) discusses at length the hagiographical elements in the Edward legends.

7 This is essentially the interpretation suggested by Keynes (1999, 54–5), coupled with Yorke's suggestion (1999, 106–8) that Aelfhere may have been implicated. It would also explain why the presumed relics of Edward examined scientifically in 1973–4 were found to belong to an older man: see below, note 16.

8 Chaney (1970, 254–5) discusses sacral kingship in the context of Edward's murder. On avenging the murder see Yorke 1999, 107–8; Keynes 1999, 49.

9 Yorke 1999, 108–9; Rollason 1983, *passim*, especially 13–14.

10 Raine 1879, 452; Fell 1971, 11–13; Kelly 1996, xiv, 118–22; see discussions by Keynes 1999, 50–3; MacDonald 2000, 27–8.

11 The best rehearsal of these arguments is by Ridyard 1988, 154–71. See also Rollason 1983; Rollason 1989, 142–4; Keynes 1999, 50–3.

12 I owe this perceptive interpretation to Ridyard 1988, 169–71 (quotation from p. 170).

13 Fell 1971, xxi–xxv; Keynes 1999, 53–4; Smith 1988; Smith 1991, 8–10, 13; MacDonald 2000, 28–9. Frank Hopton has pointed out that in the *Book of Common Prayer* (1662) Edward has the unusual distinction of two feast days.

14 Smith 1991, 14; discussed by Smith 1988; Smith 1989. The 1902–4 discovery is discussed in the report on the jar (Harden 1954) and by Sydenham (1959, 121–2), who adds the information about the 'pebble'. This

was apparently not known to Harden. See also RCHM 1972, 58, where the jar is identified with William of Malmesbury's description.

15 This and the following paragraphs (to the end of the chapter) depend heavily on press cuttings and photocopies contained in two box files (E and G) in Shaftesbury Abbey Museum Library. Specific references are identified in this and the following notes. Claridge, undated, 6–7; *Times*, 27 Jan, 1931; *Western Gazette*, 30 Jan, 1931.

16 Rahtz 1989; Stowell 1970; *Times*, 24 Sept 1984 (letter from Richard Gem); Wilson 1986; Claridge 1995, 9–10; Keynes 1999, 54–5.

17 Rahtz 1989; Wilson 1986; Claridge 1995, 10.

18 Claridge 1995, 12; Rahtz 1989; Wilson 1986; various press cuttings, Sept 1984.

19 Claridge 1995, 12; *Times*, 26 Apr, 1988. Useful current information can be found on the Brookwood Cemetery Society website: www.tbcs.org.uk/edward.htm.

4 THE GLORY AND ORNAMENT OF THE TOWN

1 Aubrey and Jackson 1862, 4.

2 Hutchins 1868, 32. This chapter relies heavily on the researches of Frank Hopton, both published (Hopton 1993) and unpublished, in his manuscript history of Shaftesbury Abbey. I am deeply indebted to him.

3 Sydenham 1959, 14; RCHM 1972, 58–61; Newman and Pevsner 1972, 362–3; Keen 1999, 7–8; Miller 1999, 165–72; Rutter 2000. The 1108 date seems to be derived from a gloss in the Winchester Psalter (which passed in the thirteenth century to Shaftesbury Abbey). Against 14 April it claims (in Latin) that the dedication in honour of the

assumption of the Blessed Virgin Mary was celebrated by Anselm (Wormald 1973, 108, 112). Since Anselm returned from exile in late 1106, and was at London or Windsor on 14 April 1107 (Easter), and on his deathbed in April 1109 (Southern 1972, 139–43), the only available year is 1108. But the gloss must be later than 1257 (Wormald 1973, 125), 150 years or more after the event, and I can find no other reference in works about Anselm to his visiting Shaftesbury during this period.

⁴ Quote from Morris 1989, 276. Local context: Thurlby 2001. Old Sarum: RCHM 1980, 15–24, especially plan on p. 17. Comparative size: Keen 1999, 7–8. It is of course possible that Wilton Abbey church, completed 1065, was even larger; it was said to rival Westminster Abbey: Crittall 1956, 232. Nor can we be sure how far west of the excavated area the nave of Shaftesbury Abbey continued.

⁵ Keen 1999, 11; Thorn 1983, nos. 19: 13–14; Williams 1999, 131–3; Williams 1985, 225–6; Cooke 1990, 33; Sydenham 1959, 14. For the *Passio* see above, chapter 3, note 6.

⁶ RCHM 1972, 61; Emden 1977, 27–30; Eames 1980, 55–6; unpublished work by Elinor Murphy and Sheila Himmel in Shaftesbury Abbey Museum library. I am grateful to Elinor Murphy for her comments on this paragraph.

⁷ Quotation with the author's permission from Frank Hopton's unpublished history of Shaftesbury Abbey.

⁸ RCHM 1972, 58–9. Newman and Pevsner 1972, 363 date the crypt to the thirteenth century. The fourteenth–century alterations may have given rise to a dispute in 1317: see below, chapter 5, note 20.

⁹ Liturgical changes: RCHM 1972, 59. Poverty caused by excess nuns: Power 1922, 212–16; Platt 1984, 96–8. Wilton: Crittall 1956, 234. Shaftesbury quotation: Calthrop

1908a, 76; cf. Sydenham 1959, 37 for a crisis in 1267.

¹⁰ RCHM 1972, 64, with plan; also pl. 58, where it appears in the background of the 16th–century sketch. See also Hutchins 1868, 49–52; Sydenham 1959, 48–9, 80–1; *PDNHAS*, vol. 100, (1978), 116–17. Malmesbury: Freeman and Watkin 1999, 85.

¹¹ RCHM 1972, 59; Hopton 1993, 4–5. The similarity with Malmesbury, where the cloister also occupied a constricted site away from the town and overlooking a precipice, is striking. For an overview of nunnery plans see Gilchrist 1994, 92–170; Gilchrist 1995, 118–48.

¹² Hopton 1993. The surveys are published in Straton 1909, 487, 516; Hutchins 1774, 21–2.

¹³ Hopton 1993, 6. Frank Hopton has pointed out to me that the Broad Hall is probably to be identified with the 'great tenement' paying a large rent of 40s., which is referred to after the New Inn in the Pembroke survey. For monastic inns see Pantin 1961.

¹⁴ Hopton 1993, 8–10. The functions of nuns and officials are further described in chapter 5, below.

¹⁵ Hopton 1993, 10–12. Frank Hopton has, however, subsequently revised his opinion about the position of the 'work' buildings, and has kindly supplied me with an updated plan; this is similar to that displayed in the abbey museum. Brief excavation note in *PDNHAS* vol. 119, 1998, 168–9. For a good general discussion of such buildings see Aston 2000, 101–24. There is still a Laundry Lane in this area.

¹⁶ Charters and documents: Mayo 1889, 2–3; Penn 1980, 85. The topographical development of medieval Shaftesbury has been little studied: see Penn 1980, 84–90, whose plans offer the potential for detailed

analysis. High Street excavation: Border Archaeology 2001. For a summary of recent archaeological work in the Bell Street area, and a report on the excavation of a site which remained open until the seventeenth century, see Valentin and Robinson 2001.

5 GENTLE MODESTY, GRACIOUS AUSTERITY

[1] The will is printed in full, without translation, by Timmins 1994, 31–2 (no. 121). See *ibid* 29–31 (nos. 113–14, 118–20) for the bishop's response. Smith and London (2001, 606) date the will May 1393, but Timmins alters this to May 1394, presumably on the basis that the 32nd year of her reign (stated in the will) would have run from July 1393 – July 1394. Other details of Formage's reign in Hutchins 1868, 28–9; Calthrop 1908a, 78; Sydenham 1959, 52–3. Some topics are discussed further, below. For help with interpreting the will I am most grateful to Dr Corin Corley.

[2] Power 1922, 240–54; Legge 1950; Bell 1995, 66–79

[3] Giffard's apocalypse: Rhys 1946, superseding Fox 1913; discussed by Legge 1950, 106–7, and Bell 1995, 167–8. The work exists as a copy now in the Bodleian Library, Oxford.

[4] Listed and described in Bell 1995, 163–8; see also Keen 1999, 9–10; Keynes 1999, 56–8; Sydenham 1959, 61–2; Power 1922, 242–3.

[5] Bell 1995, 164–5.

[6] The literature about Marie is vast, and can best be accessed via the website of the International Marie de France Society (www.people.vcu.edu/~cmarecha/). Papers touching directly on Abbess Marie of Shaftesbury are Fox 1910, Fox 1911, Bullock-Davies 1965. See also Mickel 1974, 16–21;

Burgess and Busby 1986, 16–19; Burgess 1995, viii–ix. Elinor Murphy has commented to me that Marie's writing career seems to have moved from the youthful *Lais* in 1155–60, to the fables of her middle age, and religious subjects (*The Purgatory of St Patrick*, after 1189) when older; a chronology which would fit neatly with Marie, abbess of Shaftesbury, who held office from the 1170s until about 1215.

[7] Quoted in Power 1922, 243.

[8] Fröhlich 1994, 167–8 (no. 403). See also Fröhlich 1993, 102–3 (no. 183); Fröhlich 1994, 63–5 (no. 337).

[9] In general see Lawrence 1984, 97–124. Disturbance in 1311: Flower and Dawes 1934, vol. 1, 398–9; Disturbance in 1367: *Cal. Pat. Rolls* 1364–7, 402–3. A consequence of this event was that the altar was moved to Holy Trinity.

[10] Hutchins 1868, 35; Sydenham 1959, 48. An entry in the Patent Rolls (*Cal. Pat. Rolls* 1345–8, 78) implies that the initial intention was changed in 1346, the endowment was strengthened and the chapel built in the charnel house of the nun's cemetery.

[11] *Cal. Pat. Rolls* 1485–94, 369; 1494–1509, 63–4, 142–4; Hutchins 1868, 36.

[12] Timmins 1994, 31–2. The will envisages that the priest would have a bed, with mattress, blankets, sheets and a blue coverlet permanently installed in the church. But the will was annulled. Abbess Formage also received a 40–year obit in Salisbury Cathedral: Hutchins 1868, 27; Sydenham 1959, 54.

[13] *ibid.* Nicholas Thurmond occurs in several documents as Nicholas Formage or Thurmond, so was presumably related to the abbess (I owe this observation to Frank Hopton).

[14] Cooke 1990, 39. Agnes: Horn 1982, 200–1 (nos. 1080–1); Bartholomia: Somerset

RO DD/Cd 4 (18 Feb. 1540). I owe this latter reference to Dr Joe Bettey.

[15] Backgrounds of abbesses: Smith and London 2001, 604–6. Katherine Moleyns: Wright 1985, 69 (nos. 480–2). Old Sarum bridge: Sydenham 1959, 19. Firewood: *ibid*, 22. Elizabeth de Burgh: *ibid*, 45. Catherine of Aragon: *ibid*, 60.

[16] Timmins 1994, 30–1 (no. 119).

[17] This issue is discussed by Lucas 1983, 52–8.

[18] Flower and Dawes 1934, vol. 1, 374–5; Horn 1982, 121, 241–2 (no. 895).

[19] Timmins 1994, 21 (no. 89).

[20] 1394: Timmins 1994, 30 (no. 114). 1216–23: Sydenham 1959, 17–19; cf Smith and London 2001, 604–5. 1242–3: Sydenham 1959, 19–21. 1298: Flower and Dawes 1934, vol. 1, 14. 1317: Elrington 1963, 162–3.

[21] Smith 1991, 12.

[22] Timmins 1994, 31–2 (no. 121). For a general discussion of abbey servants see Power 1922, 150–7.

[23] Maud Cuylly: *Cal. Pat. Rolls* 1345–8, 75. Joan Bray: *Cal. Close Rolls* 1374–7, 538. Richard Knyght: *Cal. Close Rolls* 1327–30, 523. Henry Ley: *Cal. Close Rolls* 1447–54, 356–7. Juliana le Despensere: *Cal. Close Rolls* 1307–13, 328. John Goldwegge: *Cal. Pat. Rolls* 1413–16, 78. Roger de Melbury: Sydenham 1959, 44. Gatekeeper: *Cal. Pat. Rolls* 1350–4, 187.

[24] Hutchins 1868, 28; Power 1922, 144–6; Edwards 1959, 318–24.

[25] Williams 1999, 142–4; Luxford 2002; Sydenham 1959, 59–60. Claridge invented a ghost story centred on Thomas Scalis: Claridge c.1936.

6 THE BUSINESS OF A NUNNERY

[1] See chapter 2 above; Kelly 1996, xxii–xxvii; surveys transcribed in Marshall thesis.

On monastic estates generally, see Aston 2000, 125–57; and on administration by nunneries, see Coldicott 1989, 105–29.

[2] Bird 1995, 71–9; RCHM 1972, xxiv–xxvi; Geddes 2000, 183–204

[3] Kelly 1996, xxii–xxvii; Powell 1953

[4] Kelly 1996, 30–5.

[5] Williams 1968, 82–3; Thorn 1983, section 19.

[6] Transcribed from BL Harley 61, ff. 50–1, 63–5, in Marshall, thesis, 57–64, 109–19. See also Bettey 1974, 42–3; and (for those relating to Bradford on Avon) Harvey 1998.

[7] Williams 1985, *passim*, examples from pp. 230–1. This paper, and Williams 1999, offer detailed studies of the abbey's tenants in the twelfth century.

[8] Keen 1987, 26–7

[9] WRO 2667/13/530. I am grateful to Steven Hobbs for this reference. The 1381 appeal is in Sydenham 1959, 52. For casualties in Shaftesbury itself (including six priests, two chaplains and the abbess) see Fletcher 1922.

[10] Harvey and Harvey 1993 (this and the next paragraph).

[11] Hutchins 1868, 643–5

[12] Calthrop 1908a, 76; Cooke 1990, 31–2; Stevenson 1987, xxv, and 66 (228).

[13] Hutchins 1868, 35–6; Calthrop 1908a, 75.

[14] Dorset examples: RCHM 1972, 46, 114–15; Hutchins 1868, 548; Wiltshire examples: Crowley 1987, 130–1, 141, 144, 206.

[15] Dufty 1947; Platt 1969, 240–2; Crowley 1987, 198–9

[16] Haslam 1984b; English Heritage 1993

[17] Mills 1989, 160, 164, 115, etc

[18] Aston 2000, 131–2; cf. Bishopstone in the Ebble valley.

[19] Jervoise 1954

[20] Wincombe: Crowley 1987, 146. On

monastic parks in Wessex see Bond 1994,
139. Wilson (1978, 34–5) describes a third
Shaftesbury Abbey park, the 'Out–Park' in
the area north of Breach Common. But this
land belonged to Alcester Abbey and, in a
note to me, Frank Hopton has convincingly
argued against Wilson's interpretation, by
examining perambulations of the adjacent
Gillingham Forest.

7 Disintegration

[1] Hutchins 1868, 30, 468, 470; Sydenham 1959, 59–60; Calthrop 1908a, 77, 79.

[2] On aristocratic nuns, see Harris 1993;
on leasing demesnes, Hare 1981 (Wiltshire
evidence), Coldicott 1989, 112 (Hampshire
nunneries), Crowley 1987, 226 (Tisbury); on
demesne flocks, Bettey 1989, 32–4, 163–4.

[3] Cooke 1996, 288–91. Winchester
nunnery had 23 nuns in 1539, but its 1535
income was £179: Knowles and Hadcock
1953, 221.

[4] Cannington nuns: Bettey 1989, 64,
180–1.

[5] Bishop of Shaftesbury: Hutchins 1868,
8.

[6] This and the two following paragraphs
are based largely on Bettey 1992; see also
Bettey 1989; Hutchins 1868, 30–2;
Sydenham 1959, 63–7.

[7] Sources as note 6; also Youings 1971, 78.

[8] Yeatman 1882, 272–3; Webb 1916, 20–3.

[9] Yeatman 1882, 270.

[10] Yeatman, 1882, 272–3; Webb 1916, 20–
3; Hutchins 1868, 737. The lease is in WSRO
2667/3/3. A letter dated 1898 from the then
Lord Arundell filed with this document
suggests that the family was very unhappy
with the imputation that their ancestor had
been involved with the abbey prior to the
dissolution, and their position is defended

(somewhat half–heartedly) by Webb 1916,
16–18. Quotation from Bettey 1989, 16.

[11] Sydenham 1959, 66–7; Cooke 1996,
298; Baskerville 1937, 222–3. The list of nuns
is given in Dugdale 1819, 485–6; Hutchins
1868, 31–2, and Bettey 1989, 180–1.

[12] Cooke 1996, 300–1; Sydenham 1959,
67; Bettey 1989, 111; Bettey 1992, 7, citing
Straton 1909, 487 (actually on 492).

[13] Hinton Charterhouse: Bettey 1989, 122;
Arundell's house: Gerard 1980, 92; Hutchins
1868, 40, and map opp. p.1. Wright (1843)
describes the stone, tiles, timber and other
items salvaged from the abbey buildings
which were sold to local people after the
dissolution (I owe this reference to Frank
Hopton).

[14] Leland: Smith 1910, 110–11. I have
argued elsewhere (Chandler 1996, 184, note
22) that the last page of Leland's autograph of
this journey, now lost, may have been
missing when the surviving copy was made.
This could well have included a description
of Shaftesbury. The sketch of the ruined
abbey is best reproduced in RCHM 1972,
plate 58, where it is dated c. 1553.

[15] Hopton 1993. This study includes also
(as an appendix, pp. 12–13) transcripts or
translations of the three surveys, including
the 1574 passage quoted here. See also
Straton 1909, 487, 516.

8 The City of a Dream

[1] The position of the stocks and cross is
seen in a 1791 drawing in Innes 1992, 58; cf
Hutchins 1868, 42. Quotation from Hardy
1895, 249.

[2] Hardy 1895, v; Millgate 1982, 368.
Hardy probably visited Shaftesbury in
September 1894: Millgate 1982, 359. Mayo
1894, quotes from 38–9, 51. The paper was

read at Shaftesbury on 11 July 1893 (*PDNHFC* vol. 15, xxviii). Hardy appears in the Club's list of members until 1893, but not from 1894 onwards.

3 Slater 2000, 600–3; see also tables in Dyer 2000; and Sheail 1998, 83–4. The Dorchester total is from Underdown 1992, 11.

4 Botyler: Hutchins 1868, 89–90, 92; Mayo 1889, 40, 80. Cockes: Mayo 1889, 77–9 (I assume 'Tonker' is a misreading for 'Touker'). Shoil and fulling mill: Mayo 1889, 20, 38, 43, 79–81; Hutchins 1868, 19. Predi: Coleman 1961, 310. See discussion by Innes 1992, 26.

5 See above, chapters 6 and 7. On pilgrimage see Finucane 1995 191–202.

6 Mayo 1889, 3–5; Mayo 1894, 45–6. The first Guildhall is referred to in a deed of 1496 (Mayo 1889, 80 (no.71) and is located on a map of c. 1620: Hutchins 1868, 7. Part of it may survive in the footings of 1 Park Walk: Jervoise 1950, 5.

7 Mayo 1889, 36–8, 78–9 (e.g. nos. 42, 56); Hutchins 1868, 89; Lewis 1993, 212, 218; Innes 1992, 23. Another goldsmith lived in Shaftesbury in the sixteenth century: Straton 1909, 494, 517.

8 Mayo 1889, 21, 78 (no.51); Hutchins 1868, 88, 91; Calthrop 1908b, 104.

9 Gerard 1980, 91.

10 Sydenham 1959, 75–86; Penn 1980, 85; Hutchins 1868, 45–53; RCHM 1972, 61–3. St Peter's absorbed St Martin's and St Andrew's parishes; Holy Trinity absorbed St Laurence's.

11 St Peter's: Innes 1992, 44–5; Puritans: Pope 1913; Byzant ceremony: Howarth and Young 1972; Frampton 1990.

12 In general: Sydenham 1959, 87–90; Almonry: Hopton 1993, 6; St John's: Calthrop 1908b.

13 In general: Innes 1992, 39–42, citing Mayo 1889, 63–4; Sydenham 1959, 91–2. On

Matthew and Margaret Chubb, see Bettey 1991 and Underdown 1992 (quote from p. 33). Sydenham has Jane and Margaret as mother and daughter, but I assume that Bettey is correct in making them sisters.

14 Bettey 1980a, 2; Bettey 1980b, 205–6; see also Mayo 1889, 60.

15 Bettey 1980a, 2; Innes 1992, 34–5; Mills 1989, 151. Post–road, see Robertson 1961; Carriers: Gerhold 1993, 225; Coach: Hoskins 1954, 150.

16 This episode is set out at length in Mayo 1889, chapters 1 and 5.

17 Innes 1992, 39–40, drawing on Mayo 1889. One suspects that Mayo's pessimistic verdict on Shaftesbury's post–dissolution predicament (see note 2 above) was coloured by his long exposure to the litigation while cataloguing the municipal archives.

18 Derived from Meekings 1951, especially pp. 22–3, 118–22.

19 Jervoise 1950, 9; Innes 1992, 40, 43–5; Gibbon 1980.

20 Sydenham 1959, 93–5; Innes 1992, 35–6; Bettey 1980a; Bettey 1980b.

21 Taylor 1970, 188. In 1951 T W French of RCHM compiled a list of visible medieval stone fragments in Shaftesbury; his notes are in Shaftesbury Town Museum (I am indebted to Frank Hopton for this information).

9 On Removing the Rubbish

1 Hopton 1993; Sydenham 1959, 109, derived from Jervoise 1951, xxvi–xxvii. The 1615 map is reproduced in Hutchins 1868, opp. p.1.

2 Sydenham 1959, 72.

3 RCHM 1972, 71–2 (nos. 88, 89); Jervoise 1951, xix–xx; Sydenham 1959, 110–13; Rutter 1827, 42; Innes 1992, 58.

4 Jervoise 1951, xix–xx; Sydenham 1959,

110–13. The 1799 Upjohn map is in Shaftesbury Town Museum, and the relevant portion is reproduced by Hopton 1993, 6. Dyneley and Park Walk: Innes 1992, 58; Hopton 1993, 1.

[5] Hutchins 1774, 19–21; the passages relevant to early archaeological discoveries are repeated verbatim in Hutchins 1868, 32, 36, 38.

[6] Bowles 1817; Hutchins 1868, 41; Hawkins 1995, 22–3; Woodbridge 1970.

[7] Bowles 1817: part of his report is printed in Hutchins 1868, 32. In 1831 Bowles is recorded as having given away a seal dug up in Donhead: Hawkins 1995, 172. Sir Stephen Glynne visited in 1826: Glynne 1924, 51. Tout Hill wall: Jervoise 1950, 5; RCHM 1972, 75 (no. 128).

[8] Maps: DRO Ph 485 (1817); DRO T/SY (1845: the Holy Trinity and St Peter tithe map); DRO D462/1 (1848). 1861 quote: Kite 1862, 272.

[9] See the account of proceedings in *WANHM* vol. 7, 1862, 229–44.

[10] Kite 1862; Reynolds 1862; Hutchins 1868, 32–5.

[11] Reynolds 1862, 27, on extending the graveyard; Bradby 1984, on Kite; *WANHM* vol. 7, 1862, 237, 248, on Batten.

[12] Sydenham 1959, 126; DRO SYB minute book 27.3.1902, 23.5.1902. Biographical details of Doran Webb from his obituary in *WANHM* vol. 45, 1931, 618–19; his claim to Shaftesbury ancestry, *Salisbury Journal*, 11.11.1905, p.8.

[13] Full account in *Salisbury Journal*, 14.6.1902, p.6; summarised in Sydenham 1959, 118.

[14] Excavations: Webb 1903; Webb 1904; Sydenham 1959, 118–20; Claridge 1935, 23–4. Freedom ceremony: DRO SYB minute book 21.12.1903; *Salisbury Journal*, 16.12.1903.

[15] Webb 1905; DRO SYB minute book 23.3.1904, 3.8.1904, 28.9.1904; *Salisbury Journal*, 6.2.1904, p.3; 1.10.1904, p.2.

[16] *Salisbury Journal*, 5.11.1904, p.2; 11.11.1905, p.8; Claridge 1935, 24; RCHM 1972, 64.

[17] DRO SYB minute books, 3.8.1910, 9.11.1910, 14.6.1911, 7..5.1913, 21.5.1913, 4.2.1914, 6.5.1914; *Salisbury Journal*, 24.6.1911, p.2; Sydenham 1959, 122; quote from *WANHM* vol.38, 1914, 551–2.

[18] The 1918–19 sales are described by Innes 1992, 95–7. 1921 visit: *PDNHAS*, vol. 43, 1923, xlii–xliv. Scheduling: Sydenham 1959, 124–5. 1929 visit: *PDNHAS*, vol. 51, 1930, 70–1. 1930 offer to council: DRO SYB minute book, 16.7.1930. Claridge's purchase: Claridge 1935, 24.

[19] Claridge, undated; DRO SYB minute book, 13.7.1932; Fox and Sons 1951. See also chapter 3 above. The abbey museum library includes typed notes of a conversation between Bert Richards and Elinor Murphy in October 1998.

[20] Fox and Sons 1951; Sydenham 1959, 124; *PDNHAS* vol. 77, 1956, 141.

[21] Carter 1971, 20. Files and cuttings in Shaftesbury Abbey Museum library, and information from Elinor Murphy. Brief notes on excavations have been published in *PDNHAS*, vol. 113, 1992, 181; vol. 114, 1993, 238; vol. 115, 1994, 149; vol. 119, 1997, 168–9. See also Corney 2002 for a new survey of the abbey site.

Bibliography

Aston, Mick, 2000, *Monasteries in the landscape* (Stroud: Tempus)

Aubrey, John, and Jackson, J.E., 1862, *Wiltshire: the topographical collections* (Devizes: Wiltshire Arch. & Nat. Hist. Soc.)

Barnes, William 1879, *Poems of rural life in the Dorset dialect* [references are to the 1898 Kegan Paul edition)

Baskerville, Geoffrey, 1937, *English monks and the suppression of the monasteries* (London: Cape)

Bell, David N., 1995, *What nuns read: books and libraries in medieval English nunneries* (Cistercian Studies 158)

Bellinger, Aidan, 1999, 'Benedictine life and influence then and now', in Keen 1999, 117-30

Bettey, J.H., 1974, *Dorset* (Newton Abbot: David & Charles)

Bettey, J.H., 1980a, 'The marketing of agricultural produce in Dorset during the seventeenth century', *Proceedings of the Dorset Natural History and Archaeological Society*, vol. 99, 1–5

Bettey, J.H., 1980b, 'Markets and fairs in seventeenth century Dorset', *Somerset and Dorset Notes and Queries*, vol. 30, 203–6

Bettey, J.H., 1989, *The suppression of the monasteries in the west country* (Stroud: Alan Sutton)

Bettey, J.H., 1991, 'Matthew Chubb of Dorchester: rapacious moneylender and benevolent philanthropist', *Proceedings of the Dorset Natural History and Archaeological Society*, vol. 112, 1–4

Bettey, J.H., 1992, 'The suppression of the Benedictine nunnery at Shaftesbury in 1539', *Hatcher Review*, vol. 4 (32), Autumn 1992, 3–11

Biddle, Martin, 1976, 'Towns', in Wilson, David M. (ed), *The archaeology of Anglo-Saxon England*, 99–150

Bird, Eric, 1995, *Geology and scenery of Dorset* (Bradford on Avon: Ex Libris)

Bond, James, 1994, 'Forests, chases, warrens and parks in medieval Wessex', in Michael Aston and Carenza Lewis (eds.), *The medieval landscape of Wessex* (Oxbow Monograph 46), 115–58

Border Archaeology, 2001, Programme of archaeological work at the Southern Electricity Depot, High Street, Shaftesbury, Dorset [unpublished client report 2001–50LJN: copy in Dorset CC SMR]

Bowles, Charles, 1817, letter in *Gentleman's Magazine*, 1817 (i), 209

Bradby, Edward, 1984, 'Edward Kite, antiquary of Devizes (1832–1930)', *Wiltshire*

Archaeological and Natural History Magazine, vol. 78, 82–6

Breach, Bob, 1998, *Melbury Abbas: a narrative history of a Dorset parish* (Melbury Abbas: Melbury Press)

Brooks, N.P., 1964, 'The unidentified forts of the burghal hidage', *Medieval Archaeology*, vol. 8, 74–90

Bullock-Davies, Constance, 1965, 'Marie, abbess of Shaftesbury, and her brothers', *English Historical Review*, vol. 80, 314–22

Burgess, Glyn S., 1995, *Marie de France Lais* (Bristol Classical Press [text by Alfred Ewert]

Burgess, Glyn S., and Busby, Keith, 1986, *The Lais of Marie de France* (Penguin Classics)

Calthrop, M.M.C., 1908a, 'The Abbey of Shaftesbury', *Victoria History of Dorset*, vol. 2, 73–9

Calthrop, M.M.C., 1908b, 'The Hospital of St John the Baptist, Shaftesbury', *Victoria History of Dorset*, vol. 2, 103–4

Carter, Phyllis, 1971, *The ancient history of Shaftesbury and its abbey* (privately published: condensed from Sydenham 1959)

Chandler, John, 1996, 'John Leland in the west country', in Mark Brayshay (ed.), *Topographical writers in south-west England* (University of Exeter Press), 34–49, 182–5

Chaney, William A., 1970, *The cult of kingship in Anglo-Saxon England* (Manchester UP)

Claridge, J. Wilson, undated, *Report of excavations on the site of the Royal Abbey Church of Our Lady and St Eadward the Martyr at Shaftesbury, AD 1930–31* (privately published)

Claridge, J. Wilson, 1935, *The history of Shaftesbury Abbey AD 888 till AD 1935* (Shaftesbury: Pearson)

Claridge, J. Wilson, c.1936, *The ghost of Shaftesbury Abbey* (privately printed)

Claridge, J. Wilson, 1995, *The recorded miracles of St Edward the Martyr*, 2nd ed (Brookwood: St Edward Brotherhood)

Coldicott, D.K., 1989, *Hampshire nunneries* (Chichester: Phillimore)

Coleman, Olive, 1961, *The brokage book of Southampton 1443–1444*, vol. 2 (Southampton Records Series 6)

Collier, C. R., 1990, 'Romsey minster in Saxon times', *Proceedings of the Hampshire Field Club*, vol. 46, 41–52

Cooke, Kathleen, 1990, 'Donors and daughters: Shaftesbury Abbey's benefactors, endowments and nuns c.1086–1130', *Anglo-Norman Studies*, vol. 12, 29–45

Cooke, Kathleen, 1996, 'The English nuns and the dissolution', in Blair, John, and Golding, Brian (eds.), *The cloister and the world: essays in medieval history in honour of Barbara Harvey*, (Clarendon Press), 287–301

Corney, Mark, 2002, *A survey of Shaftesbury Abbey, Dorset* (AC *archaeology*, unpublished client report 3398/5/0)

Crittall, Elizabeth, 1956, 'The abbey of Wilton', *Victoria history of Wiltshire*, vol. 3, 231–42

Crowley, D.A. (ed.), 1987, *The Victoria history of Wiltshire*, vol. 13

Dufty, A.R., 1947, 'Place Farm, Tisbury', *Archaeological Journal*, vol. 104, 168–9

Dugdale, William, 1819, *Monasticon Anglicanum*, new ed., vol. 2

Dumville, David N., 1992, *Wessex and England from Alfred to Edgar* (Boydell Press)

Dutton, L.S., 1988, 'King Alfred at Shaftesbury: the location of Egbert's Stone', *Proceedings of the Dorset Natural History and Archaeological Society*, vol. 109, 141–2

Dyer, Alan, 2000, 'Ranking lists of English medieval towns', in D M Palliser (ed.) *The Cambridge urban history of Britain, vol. 1: 600–1540* (Cambridge UP), 747–70

Eames, Elizabeth, 1980, *Catalogue of medieval lead-glazed earthenware tiles in the Department of Medieval and Later Antiquities, British Museum . . .* vol. 1 (British Museum Publications)

Edwards, Kathleen, 1959, *The registers of Roger Martival, bishop of Salisbury, 1315–1330*, vol. 1 (Canterbury and York Society, vol. 55)

Ellis, Peter (ed.), 2000, *Ludgershall Castle Wiltshire: a report on the excavations by Peter Addyman, 1964–1972* (WANHS Monograph 2)

Elrington, C.R., 1963, 1972, *The registers of Roger Martival, bishop of Salisbury, 1315–1330*, vols. 2(1), 2(2) (Canterbury and York Society, vols. 57–8)

Emden, A.B., 1977, *Medieval decorated tiles in Dorset* (Phillimore)

English Heritage, 1993, *Bradford on Avon tithe barn: a short guide*

Fell, Christine E., 1971, *Edward King and Martyr* (University of Leeds: Leeds Texts and Monographs, new series)

Fell, Christine E., 1978, 'Edward King and Martyr and the Anglo-Saxon hagiographic tradition', in Hill (ed.), 1978, 1–13

Finucane, Ronald, 1995, *Miracles and pilgrims: popular beliefs in medieval England*; new ed, (Macmillan)

Fletcher, J.M.J., 1922, 'The Black Death in Dorset', *Proceedings of the Dorset Natural History and Antiquarian Field Club*, vol. 43, 1–14

Flower, C.T., and Dawes, M.C.B., 1934, *Registrum Simonis de Gandavo, dioceis Saresbiriensis, AD 1297–1315*, 2 vols. (Canterbury and York Society, vols. 40–1)

Foot, Sarah, 2000a, *Veiled women I: the disappearance of nuns from Anglo-Saxon England* (Ashgate)

Foot, Sarah, 2000b, *Veiled women II: female religious communities in England, 871–1066* (Ashgate)

Fox, J.C., 1910, 'Marie de France', *English Historical Review*, vol. 25, 303–6

Fox, J.C., 1911, 'Mary, abbess of Shaftesbury', *English Historical Review*, vol. 26, 317–26

Fox, J.C., 1913, 'An Anglo-Norman apocalypse from Shaftesbury Abbey', *Modern Language Review*, vol. 8, 338–51

Fox and Sons, 1951, *The Abbey ruins and lodge, Shaftesbury, Dorset: auction 7 June 1951* [auction catalogue in Dorchester Reference Library]

Frampton, George, 1990, 'The Shaftesbury Byzant: a south of England Morris?' *Folklore*, vol. 101, 152–61

Freeman, Jane, and Watkin, Aelred, 1999, *A history of Malmesbury* (Wiltshire County Council) [reprinted from *VCH Wilts*]

Fröhlich, Walter, 1990, 1993, 1994, *The letters of Saint Anselm of Canterbury*, 3 vols. (Cisterican Studies 96, 97, 142)

Fryde, E.B. *et al*, 1986, *Handbook of British chronology*; 3rd ed. (Royal Historical Society Guides and Handbooks 2)

Garmonsway, G. N. (ed.), 1953, *The Anglo-Saxon Chronicle* (Dent)

Geddes, Isobel, 2000, *Hidden depths: Wiltshire's geology and landscapes* (Bradford on Avon: Ex Libris Press)

Gem, Richard, 1978, 'Church architecture in the reign of King Aethelred,' in David Hill (ed.), 1978, 105–14

Gerard, Thomas, 1980, *Coker's survey of Dorsetshire* (Dorset Publishing) [reprint of 1732 edition, attributed wrongly to John Coker]

Gerhold, Dorian, 1993, *Road transport before the railways: Russell's London flying*

Waggons (Cambridge Univ. Press)

Gibbon, R.G., 1980, 'John Foyle of Shaftesbury', *Somerset and Dorset Notes and Queries*, vol. 30, 131–3

Gilchrist, Roberta, 1994, *Gender and material culture: the archaeology of religious women* (London: Routledge)

Gilchrist, Roberta, 1995, *Contemplation and action: the other monasticism* (Leicester UP)

Glynne, Stephen, 1924, 'Notes on some Dorset churches (cont.)', *Proceedings of the Dorset Natural History and Antiquarian Field Club*, vol. 45, 12–80

Hall, Teresa A., 2000, *Minster churches in the Dorset landscape* (British Archaeological Reports, British Series 304)

Harden, D.B., 1954, 'A glass bowl of Dark Age date and some medieval grave-finds from Shaftesbury Abbey', *Antiquaries Journal*, vol. 34, 188–94

Hardy, Thomas, 1895, *Jude the obscure* [references are to the 1906 Macmillan pocket edition]

Hare, J.N., 1981, 'The demesne lessees of fifteenth-century Wiltshire', *Agricultural History Review*, vol. 29, 1–15

Harris, Barbara J., 1993, 'A new look at the Reformation: aristocratic women and nunneries, 1450–1540', *Journal of British Studies*, vol. 32, 89–113

Harvey, Robert B., 1998, 'Shaftesbury Abbey's 12th-century rentals for Bradford-on-Avon', *Wiltshire Archaeological and Natural History Magazine*, vol. 91, 76–89

Harvey, R.B., and Harvey, B.K., 1993, 'Bradford on Avon in the 14th century', *Wiltshire Archaeological and Natural History Magazine*, vol. 86, 118–29

Haslam, Jeremy (ed.), 1984a, *Anglo-Saxon towns in southern England* (Phillimore)

Haslam, Jeremy, 1984b, 'Excavations at Barton Farm, Bradford on Avon, 1983:

interim report', *Wiltshire Archaeological and Natural History Magazine*, vol. 78, 120–1

Hawkins, Desmond (ed.), 1995, *The Grove diaries: the rise and fall of an English family 1809–1925* (Dovecote Press)

Hill, David (ed.), 1978, *Ethelred the Unready: papers from the millenary conference* (BAR British Series, no. 59)

Hill, David, 1967, 'The burghal hidage – Lyng', *Proceedings of the Somerset Archaeological and Natural History Society*, vol. III, 64–6

Hill, David, and Rumble, A.R., 1996, *The defence of Wessex: the Burghal Hidage and Anglo-Saxon fortification* (Manchester University Press)

Hinton, D.A., 1977, *Alfred's kingdom: Wessex and the south 800–1500* (Dent)

Hopton, F.C., 1993, 'The buildings of Shaftesbury Abbey in the mid 16th century', *Proceedings of the Dorset Natural History and Archaeological Society*, vol. 115, 1–14

Horn, Joyce M., 1982, *The register of Robert Hallum, bishop of Salisbury, 1407–17* (Canterbury and York Society, vol. 72)

Hoskins, William G., 1954, *Devon* (A New Survey of England series, Collins)

Howarth, F., and Young, J.A., 1972, *A brief history of the water supply of Shaftesbury, Dorset* (Shaftesbury & District Historical Society, publication 4)

Hutchins, John, 1774, *The history and antiquities of the county of Dorset*, 1st ed., vol.2

Hutchins, John, 1868, *The history and antiquities of the county of Dorset*, 3rd ed., vol.3

Innes, Brenda, 1992, *Shaftesbury: an illustrated history* (Dovecote Press)

Jacob, E.F., 1947, *The register of Henry Chichele, archbishop of Canterbury,*

1414–43, vol. 4 (Canterbury and York Society, vol. 47)

Jervoise, E., 1950, *Shaftesbury, Dorset: the streets, roads and lanes* (Shaftesbury & District Historical Society, publication 1)

Jervoise, E., 1951, 'Notes on Shaftesbury inns, etc, from various sources' [typescript in Dorchester Reference Library]

Jervoise, E., 1954, 'The manor of Barton, Shaftesbury', *Proceedings of the Dorset Natural History and Archaeological Society*, vol. 76, 67–73

Keen, Laurence, 1980, 'Late Saxon pottery from St Peter's Church, Shaftesbury', *Proceedings of the Dorset Natural History and Archaeological Society*, vol. 99, 129–31

Keen, Laurence, 1984, 'The towns of Dorset', in Haslam, 1984a, 203–47

Keen, Laurence, 1987, 'Medieval saltworking in Dorset', *Proceedings of the Dorset Natural History and Archaeological Society*, vol. 109, 25–8

Keen, Laurence (ed.), 1999, *Studies in the early history of Shaftesbury Abbey* (Dorset CC)

Kelly, S.E., 1996, *The charters of Shaftesbury Abbey* (Anglo-Saxon Charters, 5; Oxford UP for British Academy)

Keynes, Simon, 1993, 'George Harbin's transcript of the lost cartulary of Athelney Abbey', *Proceedings of the Somerset Archaeological and Natural History Society*, vol. 136, 149–59

Keynes, Simon, 1996, 'On the authenticity of Asser's *Life of King Alfred*', *Journal of Ecclesiastical History*, vol. 47, 529–51

Keynes, Simon, 1999, 'King Alfred the Great and Shaftesbury Abbey', in Keen 1999, 17–72

Keynes, Simon, and Lapidge, Michael (eds.), 1983, *Alfred the Great: Asser's Life of King Alfred and other contemporary sources* (Penguin Classics)

Kite, Edward, 1862, 'Recent excavations on the site of Shaftesbury Abbey', *Wiltshire Archaeological and Natural History Magazine*, vol. 7, 272–7

Knowles, David, *et al.*, 1972, *The heads of religious houses, England and Wales, 940–1216* (Cambridge UP)

Knowles, D., and Hadcock, R.N., 1953, *Medieval religious houses of England and Wales* (London: Longman)

Labarge, Margaret Wade, 1990, *A small sound of the trumpet: women in medieval life* (Hamish Hamilton)

Lawrence, C. H., 1984, *Medieval monasticism: forms of religious life in western Europe in the middle ages* (Longman)

Legge, M. Dominica, 1950, *Anglo-Norman in the cloisters* (Edinburgh UP)

Lewis, Elisabeth A., 1993, *The Southampton port and brokage books 1448–9* (Southampton Record Series 36)

Leyser, Henrietta, 1995, *Medieval women: a social history of women in England 450–1500*

Liveing, Henry G.D., 1906, *Records of Romsey Abbey* (Winchester: Warren)

Lucas, Angela M., 1983, *Women in the middle ages: religion, marriage and letters* (Harvester Press)

Luxford, Julian, 2002, 'Museum stones link to St Peter's church brass: Shaftesbury Abbey's lay officers remembered, *Friends of Shaftesbury Abbey Newsletter* Autumn/Winter 2002, 3

McAleavy, Tony, 1996, *Life in a medieval abbey* (English Heritage Gatekeeper series)

MacDonald, Jennifer, 2000, *A millennium tale of monarchs, murder, mystery and mayhem* (Wiltshire County Council)

Marshall, Lydia, undated thesis, 'The early economic history of Shaftesbury Abbey'

[typescript in WRO, includes transcripts of surveys from BL Harley 61]

Mayo, C.H., 1889, *The municipal records of the borough of Shaftesbury: a contribution to Shastonian history* (Sherborne: Sawtell)

Mayo, C.H., 1894, 'Shaftesbury', *Proceedings of the Dorset Natural History and Antiquarian Field Club*, vol. 15, 36–51

Meekings, C.A.F. (ed.), 1951, *Dorset hearth tax assessments 1662–1664* (Dorchester: Longmans)

Meyer, M.A., 1977, 'Women and the tenth century English monastic reform', *Revue Bénédictine* tom. 87, 34–61

Meyer, M.A., 1981, 'Patronage of the West Saxon royal nunneries in late Anglo-Saxon England', *Revue Bénédictine* tom. 91, 332–58

Mickel, Emanuel, 1974, *Marie de France* (New York: Twayne)

Miller, Alan, 1999, *The monasteries of Dorset* (Albemarle Books)

Millgate, Martin, 1982, *Thomas Hardy: a biography* (Oxford UP)

Mills, A.D., 1989, *The place-names of Dorset,* vol. 3 (English Place-Name Society 59/60)

Morris, Richard, 1989, *Churches in the landscape* (Dent)

Murphy, Elinor, 1992, 'Anglo-Saxon abbey Shaftesbury - Bectun's base or Alfred's foundation?', *Proceedings of the Dorset Natural History and Archaeological Society,* vol. 113, 23–32

Murphy, Elinor, 1994, 'The nunnery that Alfred built at Shaftesbury', *Hatcher Review,* vol. 4 (38), Autumn 1994, 40–53

Newman, John, and Pevsner, Nikolaus, 1972, *Dorset* (Penguin: The Buildings of England)

Okasha, Elisabeth, 1983, 'A supplement to *Handlist of Anglo-Saxon non-runic inscriptions*', *Anglo-Saxon England*, vol. 11, 83–118

Owen, G.R., 1979, 'Wynflaed's wardrobe', *Anglo-Saxon England*, vol. 8, 195–222

Pantin, W.A., 1961, 'Medieval inns', in E M Jope (ed.), *Studies in building history*, 166–91

Penn, K.J., 1980, *Historic towns in Dorset* (DNHAS Monograph series, 1)

Platt, Colin, 1969, *The monastic grange in medieval England: a reassessment* (Macmillan)

Platt, Colin, 1984, *The abbeys and priories of medieval England* (Secker & Warburg)

Pope, F.J., 1913, 'Puritans at Shaftesbury in the early Stuart period', *Somerset and Dorset Notes and Queries*, vol. 13, 160–2

Powell, W.R., 1953, 'Bradford-on-Avon', *Victoria History of Wiltshire*, vol. 7, 5–51

Power, Eileen, 1922, *Medieval English nunneries c. 1275 to 1535* (Cambridge UP)

Rahtz, Philip A., 1989, 'The bones of St Edward the Martyr', *British Archaeological News*, vol. 4 (2), March 1989, 17–18

Raine, James (ed.), 1879, *The histories of the church of York and its archbishops*, vol. 1 (Rolls Series)

RCHM, 1972, Royal Commission on Historical Monuments (England), *An inventory of historical monuments in the county of Dorset, vol.4: North Dorset*

RCHM, 1980, Royal Commission on Historical Monuments (England), *Ancient and historical monuments in the city of Salisbury, vol.1*

Reynolds, J.J., 1862, *Ancient history of Shaftesbury with some account of the excavations on the site of the ancient abbey church, 1861–62* [reprinted c.1932]

Rhys, Olwen, 1946, *An Anglo-Norman rhymed apocalypse with commentary* (Anglo-Norman Text Society, vol. 6) [introduction by Sir John Fox]

Ridyard, Susan J., 1988, *The royal saints of Anglo-Saxon England: a study of West Saxon and East Anglian cults* (Cambridge UP)

Robertson, Alan W., 1961, *Great Britain: post roads, post towns and postal rates 1635–1839* (Pinner: author)

Rollason, David W., 1983, 'The cults of murdered royal saints in Anglo-Saxon England', *Anglo-Saxon England*, vol. 11, 1–22

Rollason, David W., 1989, *Saints and relics in Anglo-Saxon England* (Blackwell)

Ross, M.S., 1993, 'Melbury Abbas: medieval pottery in perspective', *Proceedings of the Dorset Natural History and Archaeological Society*, vol. 115, 111–19

Rutter, Jan, 1986, 'Where was Shaftesbury at Domesday?', *Dorset Year Book*, 1986, 17–22

Rutter, Jan, 1990, 'The search for a small Anglo Saxon bound at Shaftesbury', *Proceedings of the Dorset Natural History and Archaeological Society*, vol. 111, 125–7

Rutter, Jan, 2000, *A guide to the church of St Mary the Holy Cross and St Edward at Shaftesbury Abbey* (Shaftesbury Abbey Museum)

Rutter, Jan, 2003, *Beneath the altar: a case for the presence of a crypt within King Alfred's monastery at Shaftesbury* (privately published)

Rutter, John, 1827, 'An historical and descriptive account of the town of Shaftesbury', part 1 [typescript in Dorchester Reference Library; contains later additions]

Schofield, John, and Vince, Alan, 1994, *Medieval towns* (Leicester UP)

Scobie, Graham, and Qualmann, Ken, 1993, *Nunnaminster: a Saxon and medieval community of nuns* (Winchester Museum Service)

Scott, Ian R., 1996, *Romsey Abbey: report on the excavations 1973–1991* (Hampshire Field Club Monograph 8)

Scott, Ian R., 2001, 'Romsey Abbey: Benedictine nunnery and parish church', in G. Keevill *et al*, *Monastic archaeology: papers on the study of medieval monasteries* (Oxbow), 150–60

SDAG, 1991, Shaftesbury and District Archaeological Group, 'The church of St Rumbold, Cann, Shaftesbury, Dorset', *Proceedings of the Dorset Natural History and Archaeological Society*, vol. 112, 33–42

Shahar, Shulamith, 1983, *The fourth estate: a history of women in the middle ages* (Longman)

Sheail, John, 1998, *The regional distribution of wealth in England as indicated in the 1524/5 lay subsidy returns*, vol. 2 (List and Index Society, special series 29)

Slater, T.R., 2000, 'The south-west of England', in D M Palliser (ed.) *The Cambridge urban history of Britain, vol. 1: 600–1540* (Cambridge UP), 583–607

Smith, A.H., 1956, *English place-name elements*, part 2 (English Place-Name Society, vol. 26)

Smith, David M., and London, Vera C.M. (eds.), 2001, *The heads of religious houses England and Wales II: 1216–1377* (Cambridge UP)

Smith, Lucy Toulmin (ed.), 1910, *The itinerary of John Leland . . .*, vol. 5 (reprinted 1964, Centaur Press)

Smith, William, 1988, 'Are these the bones of martyred king?' *Western Gazette*, 11 November 1988

Smith, William, 1989, 'Viscera vindicata', *British Archaeological News*, vol. 4 (4), May 1989, 50

Smith, William, 1991, 'Sceftonia, an early

account of Shaftesbury and its abbey by William of Malmesbury', *Hatcher Review*, vol. 4 (32), Autumn 1991, 3–18

Smyth, Alfred P., 1995, *King Alfred the Great* (Oxford UP)

Southern, R.W., 1972, *The life of St Anselm, archbishop of Canterbury, by Eadmer* (Clarendon Press)

Stafford, Pauline, 1978, 'The reign of Aethelred II, a study in the limitations on royal policy and action', in Hill (ed.), 1978, 15–46

Stevenson, Janet H. (ed.), 1987, *The Edington cartulary* (Wiltshire Record Society, 42)

Stowell, Thomas E.A., 1970, 'The bones of Edward the Martyr', *Criminologist*, vol. 5, 141–60

Straton, C.R., 1909, *Survey of the lands of William, first Earl of Pembroke*, vol. 2 (Roxburghe Club)

Sydenham, Laura, 1959, *Shaftesbury and its abbey*

Taylor, Christopher, 1970, *Dorset* (Making of the English Landscape, Hodder)

Thorn, Caroline and Frank, 1983, *Domesday Book 7: Dorset* (Chichester: Phillimore)

Thorpe, Lewis (ed.), 1966, *Geoffrey of Monmouth: the History of the Kings of Britain* (Penguin Classics)

Thurlby, Malcolm, 2001, 'Aspects of romanesque ecclesiastical architecture in Dorset. . .', , *Proceedings of the Dorset Natural History and Archaeological Society*, vol. 122, 1–19

Timmins, T.C.B., 1994, *The register of John Waltham, bishop of Salisbury, 1388–95* (Canterbury and York Society, vol. 80)

Underdown, David, 1992, *Fire from heaven: life in an English country town in the seventeenth century* (Harper Collins)

Valentin, John, and Robinson, Stephen, 2001, 'Archaeological excavation and

recording of land between 28 and 30 Bell Street, Shaftesbury, Dorset', *Proceedings of the Dorset Natural History and Archaeological Society*, vol. 122, 99–109

Webb, E. Doran, 1903, *Report . . . on the excavations on the site of the ancient abbey church of Our Lady and St Edward the Martyr for 1902* (Shaftesbury Abbey Excavation Fund)

Webb, E. Doran, 1904, *Report . . . on the excavations on the site of the ancient abbey church of Our Lady and St Edward the Martyr for 1903* (Shaftesbury Abbey Excavation Fund)

Webb, E. Doran, 1905, *Report . . . on the excavations on the site of the ancient abbey church of Our Lady and St Edward the Martyr for 1904* (Shaftesbury Abbey Excavation Fund)

Webb, E. Doran, 1916, *Notes by the 12th Lord Arundell of Wardour on the family history* (London: Longman)

Whitelock, Dorothy, 1930, *Anglo-Saxon wills* (Cambridge UP)

Williams, Ann, 1968, 'Introduction to the Dorset Domesday' and 'Translation of the text of the Dorset Domesday', *Victoria History of Dorset*, vol. 3, 1–60, 61–114

Williams, Ann, 1985, 'The knights of Shaftesbury Abbey', *Anglo-Norman Studies*, vol. 8, 214–41

Williams, Ann, 1999, 'The abbey tenants and servants in the 12th century', in Keen 1999, 131–60

Wilson, Christopher, 1986, 'The bizarre tale of King Edward's bones', *Sunday Express Magazine*, 24 August 1986, 10–15

Wilson, J.D., 1978, 'The mediaeval deer parks of Dorset XVII', *Proceedings of the Dorset Natural History and Archaeological Society*, vol. 100, 31–5

Woodbridge, Kenneth, 1970, *Landscape and antiquity: aspects of English culture at*

Stourhead, 1718–1838 (Clarendon Press)

Wormald, Francis, 1973, *The Winchester psalter* (Harvey Miller)

Wright, D.P., 1985, *The register of Thomas Langton, bishop of Salisbury, 1485–93* (Canterbury and York Society, vol. 74)

Wright, T. (ed.), 1843, *Letters relating to the suppression of the monasteries*

Yeatman, John Pym, 1882, *The early genealogical history of the house of Arundel . . . (London: Mitchell and Hughes)

Yorke, Barbara, 1989, '"Sisters under the skin"? Anglo-Saxon nuns and nunneries in southern England', in Bate, Keith (*et al*), *Medieval women in southern England* (Reading Medieval Studies 15), 95–117

Yorke, Barbara, 1995, *Wessex in the early middle ages* (Leicester UP)

Yorke, Barbara, 1999, 'Edward, king and martyr: a Saxon murder mystery', in Keen 1999, 99-116

Youings, Joyce, 1971, *The dissolution of the monasteries* (London: Allen and Unwin)

Index

This index includes people, places and selected subjects. Many places and subjects will be found grouped under headings relating to Shaftesbury and Shaftesbury Abbey. Villages and minor places are in Dorset or Wiltshire unless otherwise identified (by pre-1974 counties). The notes have not been indexed.